To Sarah Elizabeth

from

Aunt Dorothy

THE *Kate Greenaway* BOOK

THE *Kate Greenaway* BOOK

BRYAN HOLME

GALLERY PRESS

ISBN: 0-8317-5300-5

This edition published 1983 by Gallery Press, an imprint of
W.H. Smith Publishers, 112 Madison Avenue, New York,
New York 10016

Printed in Hong Kong

Title page illustrations from *Marigold Garden*.
ABOVE: From *Little Ann*.
On the half-title page and OPPOSITE, from *The English Spelling-Book*.
The capital letters with which each chapter opens also come from *The English Spelling-Book*.

Contents

The text of *The Queen of the Pirate Isle* and *The Pied Piper of Hamelin* are published in full with a selection of Kate Greenaway's illustrations; the remaining chapters contain selections of pictures and verse.

To Anne Margaret

"Afternoon Tea," Illustration for *The Girls' Own Paper*, c. 1886. (Courtesy London Borough of Camden)

SUCCESS

eople laugh at me, I am so delighted and pleased with things, and they say I see with rose-coloured spectacles. What do you think—is it not a beautiful world? Sometimes have I got a defective art faculty that few things are ugly to me?"

When Kate Greenaway wrote this to her friend Frederick Locker,* *Under the Window* had made publishing history, her name had become a household word, and the children of her "pictures and rhymes" were the darlings of the English nursery.

"Since Stothard, no one has given us such clear-eyed, soft-faced happy-hearted childhood," said Austin Dobson after viewing the exhibition of original drawings for *Under the Window* at London's Fine Arts Society in 1880, "or so poetically 'apprehended' the coy reticences, the simplicities, and the small solemnities of little people. Added to this," continued the poet who was to collaborate with Kate Greenaway on two features in the *Magazine of Art* in 1883, "the old-world costume in which she usually elects to clothe her characters lends an arch piquancy of contrast to their innocent rites and ceremonies."

* Author of *London Lyrics* and known also as Frederick Locker-Lampson.

From *Under the Window.*

The twelve Miss Pelicoes
  Of course, to school were sent;
Their parents wished them to excel
  In each accomplishment.

The twelve Miss Pelicoes
  Were twelve sweet little girls;
Some wore their hair in pigtail plaits,
  And some of them wore curls.

Even in France, a country seldom given to superlatives where English art, let alone English *couture,* is concerned, *Under the Window,* or *La Lanterne Magique* as the French and Belgian publishers had called the book, was acclaimed for its originality, and the author, equally, for her understanding of children and the elegant way she dressed and drew them.

So strong was Kate Greenaway's artistic power that occasional weaknesses in her drawing and verse—a wayward foot here, a mixed metaphor or faulty rhyme there—merely added to the quaintness of a style an enraptured France called *Greenawisme.*

Here was a new *tête d'école,* said Paris, adopting Kate Greenaway's charmingly adapted end-of-the eighteenth-century frocks and smocks, aprons and bonnets, wide hats, long sleeves and long breeches, dainty ribbons and bows as its own *jeune mode.*

Shortly, *La Vie de Paris* was to report: "The graceful mode of *Greenawisme* has gained the Provinces." And we read of an English guest of the Jules Bretons who, at the end of a carriage ride through the Normandy countryside, found the artists' children—every one of them—dressed in Greenaway costumes. "They alone fit children and sunshine," explained a happy Breton to a surprised but enchanted visitor as the young darted hither and yon; "they only are worthy of beautifying the *chef d'oeuvres du bon Dieu.*"

The *Journal des Débats* thanked Kate Greenaway for more practical reasons. Before her "there had been no author and artist for the boy citizens whose trousers were always too short, and for the girl citizens whose hands are too red."

One of Kate Greenaway's more serious admirers, M. Ernest Chesneau, with the tact, delicacy, and floweriness of language the French have at such easy command, wrote in *La Peinture Anglaise:* "Miss Greenaway, with a profound sentiment of love for children, puts the child alone on the scene, companions him in all his solitudes, and shows the infantine nature in all its naïveté, its gaucherie, its touching grace, its shy alarm, its discoveries, ravishments, embarrassments and victories; the stumblings of it in wintry ways, the enchanted smiles of its spring-time and all the

From *Under the Window.*

> O ring the bells! O ring the bells!
>   We bid you, sirs, good morning;
> Give thanks, we pray,—our flowers are gay,
>   And fair for your adorning.

history of its fond heart and guileless egoism." With a Gallic thrust, M. Chesneau then added: "From the honest but fierce laugh of the coarse Saxon, William Hogarth, to the delicious smile of Kate Greenaway, there has passed a century and a half. Is it the same people which applauds today the sweet genius and tender malices of the one, and which applauded the bitter genius and slaughterous satire of the other? After all, that is possible—the hatred of vice is only another manifestation of the love of innocence. . . ."

On home ground, from the distinguished "Saxon" John Ruskin, a gentleman with whom Miss Greenaway had recently struck up a friendship and with whom she was to continue to correspond at Brantwood until his dying day in 1900, came one of the prettier bouquets: "You have the radiance and innocence of reinstated infant divinity showered again among the flowers of English meadows." And on a separate occasion Mr. Ruskin wrote, "You are fast becoming—I believe you are already, except only Edward B. Jones—the helpfullest in showing me that there are yet living souls on earth who can see the beauty and peace and Goodwill among men—and rejoice in them." And again, "Holbein lives for all time with his grim and ugly 'Dance of Death'; a not dissimilar and more beautiful immortality may be in store for you if you worthily apply yourself to produce a 'Dance of Life.' "

And some months after their first meeting in 1882, said Mr. Ruskin to Miss Greenaway, "I'm in great happiness today thinking that M. Chesneau must have got that lovely 'Kate' this morning and be in a state words won't express the ecstasy of. . . . As we've got so far as taking off hats, I trust we may in time get to taking off just a little more—say, mittens—and then—perhaps—even shoes!—and (for fairies) even stockings—and then—"

Illustration from *A Painting Book*. The coloured drawing originally appeared in *Under the Window*.

For a woman so admired, so successfully established in her chosen field, still only in her early thirties, relatively prosperous and in good health, few indeed could be her reasons not to have been, as she wrote Frederick Locker, "delighted and pleased with things."

And concerning those "rose-coloured spectacles," Kate Greenaway's was a romantic age, the outgrowth of Burns and Keats and Shelley, of nostalgia for painted ruins in deserted landscapes; a time when ugliness, theoretically at least, was as taboo as prettiness is today; when *la vie en rose*, far from being frowned upon, was the accepted thing.

While Kate Greenaway's heydays started in 1878, the year of *Under the Window*, those of Victorian England, the only beautiful world she knew and to which she and her work so utterly and completely belonged, had begun when she was a child. And they continued with more ups than downs, through to the end of the great Queen's reign.

From *Marigold Garden*.

Oh, Susan Blue,
How do you do?

From an original Greenaway drawing in Keats House. (Courtesy London Borough of Camden)

BACKGROUND

atherine Greenaway, as Kate was christened but never called, was born on March 17, 1846 at 1, Cavendish Street, Hoxton, London. She was the second daughter of John Greenaway, a draughtsman and engraver, and of Elizabeth Greenaway, a Miss Jones before the marriage. Their first-born, Lizzie, was nearly six years old at the time. There were two more Greenaways to come: Frances Rebecca (Fanny) in 1850, and Alfred John in 1852.

Kate Greenaway's birthday fell on St. Patrick's Day, a coincidence her more ardent Irish fans have tried to find significant. But the Greenaways were not Irish; the only blood in Kate that wasn't English came from a Welsh grandfather on her mother's side. Nor is there a known Catholic background. "I am very religious, though people may not think it," said Miss Greenaway late in life, "but it is in my own way."

Of small account, but oddly interesting too, was the closeness of the birthdate of Kate Greenaway and Randolph Caldecott, her chief rival-to-be on the nursery bookshelf, and an admiring friend. "There must have been some peculiar conjunction of the stars and planets in March 1846," wrote the author of *Rabbit Hill*, Robert Lawson, in *The New York Times* exactly a century later, "for in that month, less than a week apart, were born two illustrators who were to bring to children more joy and beauty than had ever been offered them in books since books began. . . . Whatever the influence, that week in March was to change the whole future of children's books."

Those who take their astrology seriously say the "less than a week apart" placed the five-day-older Miss Greenaway under the sun sign of Pisces, the Fish, and pushed the jovial author of *A Frog He Would A-Wooing Go* and other bedtime frolics over the cusp into Aries, the sign of the Ram.

OVERLEAF: From *Almanack for 1884* by Kate Greenaway

1884.]   JANUARY   **[31 Days.**

AQUARIUS   ♒   *The Water-Bearer.*

1884.]   FEBRUARY.   **[29 Days.**

PISCES   ♓   *The Fishes.*

1884.]   MARCH.   **[31 Days.**

ARIES   ♈   *The Ram.*

1884.]   APRIL.   **[30 Days.**

TAURUS   ♉   *The Bull.*

1884.]   MAY.   **[31 Days.**

GEMINI   ♊   *The Twins.*

1884.]   JUNE.   **[30 Days.**

CANCER   ♋   *The Crab.*

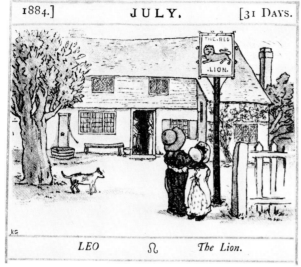

LEO   ♌   *The Lion.*

SCORPIO   ♏   *The Scorpion.*

VIRGO   ♍   *The Virgin.*

SAGITTARIUS   ♐   *The Archer.*

LIBRA   ♎   *The Balance.*

CAPRICORNUS   ♑   *The Goat.*

Without benefit of stars or palms, Miss Greenaway's definitive biographers, M. H. Spielmann and C. S. Layard, described Kate as sincere, modest, patient, intelligent, bighearted, exquisitely sensitive, forgiving, humorous, and possessing an indomitable will. She also impressed those who knew her as being very small and of dark complexion.

It is doubtful that Miss Greenaway or Mr. Caldecott would have given more than passing thought to astrology, a subject in their day almost solely the province of gypsies and the caravan. Yet she must have done some homework before illustrating the zodiac in her *Almanack for 1884*. This was the second, and in the opinion of many, the best of the seven little annuals she created.

Looking at the children in that tiny *Almanack* (pages 14 and 15), or, for that matter, looking at almost any Greenaway drawing, one cannot help wondering if ever she had imagined herself dressed in the fashion that became synonymous with her name. The same stamp of dainty, stylish perfection is recognizably hers in every figure she drew. None of her numerous imitators—Constance Haslewood, H. H. Emmerson, George Lambert, T. Pym, and K. Terrell, for example—came near to equalling it.

Outwardly, it would seem Kate Greenaway paid little attention to her appearance. "Small and plainly dressed," commented Walter Crane, the dean of nursery-book illustrators. These two artists, Greenaway and Crane, who, with a third, Caldecott, were habitually linked in publicity as the best-selling children's authors, met only once—at a play in which Lionel Tennyson, a son of the poet laureate and a friend of Miss Greenaway, was starring. The rest of Crane's impressions of Kate Greenaway that day, as related by Mr. Spielmann, were of "a very quiet and unobtrusive personality, . . . self-contained, reserved, with a certain shrewdness."

On a weekend in 1868 when Randolph Caldecott and Kate Greenaway were guests at the country house of mutual friends, Caldecott sat down and, after making this quick sketch, jokingly remarked, "I have lost *all* powers working in my own style, everything comes out Kate Greenaways."

Whatever else may be said, certainly Kate Greenaway's taste for "dressing up" found its major expression at the drawing board, as in her childhood it had through her love of dolls. Her collection of these treasures was large and as varied as her tiny budget permitted. Most of the dolls cost Kate a week's allowance, the—to her—vast sum of a farthing. Others came "horribly much dearer," Queen Victoria and Prince Albert, for instance, commanding a royal penny the pair! The delicious prospect of dressing her latest acquisition sent Kate scurrying to the collection of discarded family clothing where, from old ribbons and odd bits of this and that, she would create a dress or a hat. For plumage, a few pretty feathers could be puffed out of a pillow when her mother's head was turned another way.

Dolls in her early collection. BELOW: A sketch for *The English Spelling-Book*. BELOW RIGHT: Dolls from her *Book of Games*.

Dolls were among her most treasured memories of Highbury, the London district to which the family had moved prior to John's birth in 1852. The Highbury house was already the fifth home Kate had known, including the farm at Rolleston, Nottinghamshire, where a great-aunt, Mrs. Wise, lived and where Kate had spent a happy year or so after being "put out to nurse," due to her mother's illness.

After the Cavendish Street house had come one on Napier Street, also in Hoxton. The Greenaways lived there until the bankruptcy of a publisher indebted to John for a large engraving job left him penniless, in debt, and looking for work. So it was that the hard-pressed family pulled up stakes again and moved to Islington. Their new home was the middle of a large, rambling

From *The English Spelling-Book*.

Farm at Rolleston, painted on one of her frequent visits to Nottinghamshire as a young girl.

Elizabethan mansion, with two wings, one on either side, converted into separate living units. Each unit had a shop at street level. To the children, the building was "a very castle of romance . . . with rambling passages, several unused rooms, too dilapidated for habitation, and weird, mysterious passages which led dreadfully to nowhere"—except inevitably to some hair-raising games of hide-and-seek!

Hide-and-seek.
From her *Book of Games.*

From *The English Spelling-Book.*

An underlying reason for the Islington move had been Elizabeth Greenaway's thought to open a "fancy goods" shop and earn money to help the family through this difficult period. Her dispensing of lace, children's dresses, and other saleable items prospered, and in 1851, with John on the way, the idea of both larger living quarters and a larger shop seemed indicated. Hence to Highbury in 1852, where the family remained for more than twenty years.

It was at Highbury that Kate discovered that she could read. When she was six, the dim view she had hitherto held of her sister Lizzie's dog-eared old paperbacks brightened. Suddenly her limited world had gained a new dimension; every fairy tale she could now beg, borrow, or buy she would read and reread again and again. *Beauty and the Beast, Diamonds and Toads* (an edition of which she was to illustrate in 1871), *Cinderella,* and *Sleeping Beauty* were stories she seemed never to tire of, and as for *Bluebeard* (an edition of which she was also to illustrate in 1871), the terror and delight of those pages became a nightly experience for months! "How I used to be thrilled by 'Sister Anne, Sister Anne,' done by the servants in the agonized voice of Bluebeard's wife, and I could hardly breathe when the stains would not come off the key."

"These wonderful little books they used to sell in coloured covers, a penny and a halfpenny each," Kate remembered in the 1890s, "they were condensed and dramatic." She also observed, "Children often don't care a bit about books people think they will . . . they often like grown-up books—at any rate, I did. From the Kenny Meadows pictures to Shakespeare I learnt all the plays when I was very young indeed." She was precocious enough to be taken to and to enjoy *Henry V* —at Sadler's Wells—before she was seven.

Besides lines from Shakespeare, she learned others by heart too, but never poems with sad endings. She hated those. *How Horatius Kept the Bridge* was a favorite—"I loved that," she said —and *The Wreck of the Hesperus* and Robert Browning's *The Pied Piper of Hamelin*. The famous illustrated edition of *The Pied Piper* Kate Greenaway was to undertake after knowing the poet. It was one of her last major works, and it appeared in 1888, a year before Browning died.

A very different "delicious delight" had concerned her father on one of those days he returned from Fleet Street with an engraving job to be finished overnight; usually this was for a topical story in the *Illustrated London News*. As John Greenaway worked through till dawn, the thrill of Kate's young life would be to steal downstairs while her mother, Lizzie, Fanny, and little John were fast asleep, and make tea and toast. Then, feeling very grown-up indeed, she would share the early breakfast alone with her father.

A strong bond existed between father and daughter. He had nicknamed her "Knocker" because when she cried her face used to look like one—or so he had teasingly told her. As soon as Kate's fingers had strength enough to hold a pencil, John Greenaway had encouraged her to draw —and this he continued to do up to and through her student years. After that he watched proudly as his daughter's books, one after another, became international successes, as her paintings were accepted and shown by the Royal Academy, and as her increasing fame even led her through the gates of Buckingham Palace to tea.

There were parties in the Highbury days, too. A Mrs. D's Twelfth Night "afternoon" with its magic lantern show, followed by tea and a gigantic cake, was vividly remembered; even more so a dance at the house of Lizzie's music teacher, where the young brother of a girl Kate admired was the cause of her one triumph.

"Just this little boy—among all the girls—and tea over and dancing about to begin, the boy was led to the middle of the room . . . and told out of all the girls to choose his partner for the first dance. He took his time—looked slowly round the room, weighing this and that, and, to my utter discomfiture and dire consternation, he chose me—moment of unwished triumph—short-lived also, for he didn't remain faithful, but fell a victim later on to the wiles of some of the young ladies nearly twice his age."

Drawing for *The Ladies' Home Journal*.

From *Marigold Garden*.

Local excitement was to be found in the nearby park, where the young Greenaways might play leap frog, watch others bowl hoops, spin tops, or fly kites. Within bounds, too, was Wellington Street where they would stop to watch the Punch and Judy show, enjoying these giddiest of proceedings with shrieks of delight until the man with a hat came round for money and they had to bolt because they hadn't any.

From *Under the Window.*

Kites. From her *Book of Games.*

Sometimes their parents would take them to the Polytechnic or to the Crystal Palace, and occasionally to the theatre, the greatest treat of all. Habitually on Sundays the family went for a walk on Hampstead Heath, weather permitting. Weather not permitting, indoor pastimes included books, dolls, drawing, and combing the pages of the *Illustrated London News* to learn what might be happening in the world beyond Islington.

It is more than possible that one of these excursions to the Crystal Palace included the Great Exhibition of 1851. Lizzie would have been old enough to be taken, possibly little Kate. This major expression of industrial progress and contemporary taste—Prince Albert's idea—was opened by the Queen to unprecedented hurrahs from the press. Today it has been referred to as "a triumphant expression of British supremacy and middle-class prosperity"; then it seemed merely "triumphant."

England, pioneer of industrial revolution, was beginning to reap its monetary benefits, not, however, without casting a sad eye at the path of progress—the pitiful carving up of farm and garden lands by expanding railroads, factories, and housing developments, most of them ill-planned and ungainly.

The first signal of distress had gone up in 1848, when the Pre-Raphaelite Brotherhood was formed by William Holman Hunt, John Everett Millais, and Dante Gabriel Rossetti. This trio of artists protested the ravages of modern industry, but their plea for a return to simplicity, sincerity,

21

and respect for nature had no bearing beyond the immediate world of British art. Yet in that world, within a decade, they became gods.

Their style of painting, harking back to the precepts of the early Italian masters, was endorsed by John Ruskin—the first noted critic to do so—in *The Times*. Ruskin maintained their work to be "in finish of drawing and splendour of colour, the best in The Royal Academy."

Long before she became a friend of Ruskin, Kate Greenaway was influenced by the Pre-Raphaelites, particularly Rossetti. Practically every art student in England from the 1850s onward was. "How I should like to live always in a room with two or three Rossettis on the walls, she said in 1898. And about Millais: "His 'Ophelia' is my dearest loved English painting . . . the greatest picture of modern times." Kind words she also had for Hunt, particularly for his early work, such as "The Two Gentlemen from Verona." "I have often seen this early one, and I love it. It really is so beautiful to see such pictures," she wrote Ruskin after one of her frequent rounds of the London art galleries and museums. And as for the younger artist, Edward Burne-Jones, a Pre-Raphaelite in spirit and the most popular English painter of his day, "his drawings are *so* beautiful. . . . The large painting of King Arthur of Avalon . . . I should like to have it for a week hung opposite to me that I might know it all—every bit."

Kate Greenaway's art training had been decided when she was twelve. Prior to that her formal education had been spasmodic, to say the least. Girls' schools were few and hard to find, and a school qualifying as good, inexpensive, and close at hand, which her parents sought, simply did not exist.

First Kate had gone to a nursery school in Islington where an aged Mrs. Allaman, wearing an apron, scarf, and large frilly white cap, taught a stern A, B, C, and, worse, how to sew, tapping an admonitory thimble on this or that diminutive head whenever a pupil's stitchery displeased her.

On a letter to Lily Evans, daughter of Edmund Evans who engraved and printed most of Kate Greenaway's best books. LEFT: From *Under the Window*.

From *Marigold Garden.*

A succession of unsatisfactory teachers followed: first a Miss Jackson, who lasted for a few days, then a Miss Varley, who lasted a few weeks. Next there was Anne Fiveash, whose cross-eye filled Kate with such terror that the first lesson was over before it ever began. Following this, an arrangement was made with a lady, of unknown name, who dropped in once or twice a week to teach a little French and music. A year or two drifted past, and for lack of a better alternative it was back to Miss Fiveash, whom an older Kate suffered, if not gladly.

Meanwhile Kate Greenaway had become increasingly interested in drawing. Not only were people her subjects; she adored flowers, both the wild and the cultivated. Flowers had become a passion during her first country days at Rolleston, and so they always remained. "You can go into a beautiful new country," she remarked to her friend Violet Dickinson, "if you stand under a large apple tree and look up to the blue sky through the white flowers." And on another occasion: "I have such a wild delight in cowslips and apple blossoms—they always give me some strange feeling of *trying* to *remember,* as if I had known them in a former world." Nowhere was Kate Greenaway to depict flowers better than in her illustrations for *A Day in a Child's Life* (1881) and *Language of Flowers* (1884).

In 1857 a new phase in her work had been brought on by stories of the Indian Mutiny. "We knew all about it from the *Illustrated London News. . . .* I could sit and think of the sepoys till I could be wild with terror. . . . I was always drawing the ladies, nurses, and children escaping. Mine always escaped." So too, unfortunately, did Kate's drawings. She drew them on slate and would wipe one off to make room for another.

Within the year her parents were of the opinion that Kate would be better off training to be an artist than continuing to dillydally with teachers like Anne Fiveash. Thus began a ten-year period of hard and fruitful work, most of it at the National Art Training School in the South Kensington Museum, now the Royal College of Art.

"She and I were keen competitors," remembered a fellow South Kensington student, Elizabeth Thompson, later Lady Butler, but "very good friends . . . in spite of our rivalry. She was a very quiet student . . . peaceable . . . well-liked," and happy. For her decorative work Kate Greenaway won the Bronze Medal in 1861, the National Medal in 1864, and the Silver in 1869. Realizing her weakness in anatomy, however, she decided to add life classes at Heatherly's to her South Kensington studies. Later she also attended evening classes at the new Slade School when it first opened under the noted artist Alphonse Legros.

Design of conventional floral orna-
ment for textiles (Courtesy The Vic
ttoria and Albert Museum, London)

Drawing from one of her early sketchbooks.
(Courtesy Detroit Public Library)

Eventually Kate arrived at the stage, familiar to most students, when it became crucial to prove to herself that years of intensive—and expensive—study had been to some avail. Apart from recognition, she also wanted to contribute to her keep, the family never having been at all well-off. It had been only through her mother's enterprise and thrift that Kate had been able to study art, that Lizzie could have attended the Royal Academy of Music, and that John was to pursue his bent at the Royal College of Chemistry.

Kate Greenaway's first real break came in 1868 when she took some samples of her work along to The Dudley Gallery in the old Egyptian Hall, Picadilly. To her supreme delight, the proprietor saw sufficient promise in her selection to retain one watercolour, *Kilmeny*, and a frame of six small drawings of sprites and gnomes on wood. The drawings shortly found themselves in a black-and-white show at Dudley's, where they were spotted and quickly spoken for by the Reverend W. J. Loftie, editor of *People's Magazine*. Mr. Loftie was of a mind to print each drawing in a separate issue of his publication, accompanying it with a poem written by a leading contributor. Four of the drawings so appeared in fairly short order and the remaining two in 1873, by which time the days of the magazine were all but done.

Directly and indirectly through The Dudley Gallery, Mr. Loftie, and her father, Kate obtained a considerable amount of free-lance work. She made great friends with Mr. Loftie and his wife after visiting them at their house in Upper Berkeley Street. It was to Loftie at the end of the 1870s that Kate was to tell her famous tale concerning the fashion she had started. Laughingly she greeted him at some Bond Street exhibition at which they had met, saying: "The lady who has just left me has been staying in the country and has been to see her cousins. I asked if they were growing up as pretty as they promised. 'Yes,' she replied, 'but they spoil their good looks, you know, by dressing in that *absurd* Greenaway style'—quite forgetting that she was talking to me!"

That style, based partly on memories of quaint behind-the-times country clothes and sunbonnets at Rolleston, and partly on Kate's delightful fancy, had already emerged in the valentine cards she began designing a year or two after the exhibition at Dudley's.

Messrs. Marcus Ward & Company, who had commissioned these valentines and who later asked her to design birthday, Christmas and New Year's cards, had their headquarters in Belfast, but also a convenient office in London. At the outset of this association, which was to last approximately six years, Mr. William Marcus Ward unhesitatingly destroyed Kate's work when he thought it bad, and was equally stern, but usually quite helpful, in showing ways through which her technique could be expected to improve.

Like every intelligent artist, Kate Greenaway was always open to constructive criticism, but didn't much like being told by Mr. Ward that her early efforts at rhyming were "rubbish and without any poetic feeling." She politely disregarded unhelpful advice, or advice she knew she could not follow, including, at a later date, some she received gratuitously in letters from her great friend and mentor, John Ruskin, whose opinions were apt to reflect the mood or state of health in which he happened to awake.

Drawing from one of her early sketchbooks. (Courtesy Detroit Public Library)

In addition to the greeting cards, Marcus Ward published calendars and a dozen or more books containing Kate Greenaway's illustrations. Over the years hitherto unknown books containing one or more Greenaway illustrations have turned up in the rare-book market. The earliest so far known is *The Fairy Spinner* by Miranda Hill, published in 1875. Probably the best known is *The Quiver of Love: A Collection of Valentines* by Walter Crane and Kate Greenaway, which was put together with the friendly aid of W. J. Loftie in 1876. In *The Quiver of Love* four unidentified examples are by Greenaway—the frontispiece, "Do I Love You," "Surprise," and "Disdain"; the rest, a larger selection, are Crane's. Surprisingly, practically no characteristic difference is discernible between the two artists' work in this early, rather crudely printed work.

Another Marcus Ward project, entirely illustrated by Kate Greenaway, was *Topo: A Tale About English Children in Italy*. Lady Colin Campbell, who wrote the book long before she married Sir Colin and under the pen name of G. E. Brunefille, sold the world rights to the text for an unbelievable five pounds. So pleased was Marcus Ward with the result that "they sent me ten pounds," said a delighted Lady Campbell, "which I should think was the only case on record of a publisher doubling the price in the author's favour without being asked." The extent of Kate

Cards designed for Messrs. Marcus Ward & Co. Her early work was unsigned. Later it was characteristic of her to sign it just with her initials —K.G.

Illustration for *Diamonds and Toads.*

"Surprise." One of the four Greenaway valentine designs in *The Quiver of Love* (1876).

Greenaway's bounty for contributing the forty-four black-and-white illustrations to *Topo* is not recorded, but likely it wasn't much more, possibly much less. Actually she made only forty-three illustrations; after a long and fruitless tussle with a donkey, she gave that drawing to someone else to finish.

Kate Greenaway's earliest free-lance work also included odd jobs for Messrs. Kronheim and Company, the giant colour printers of Shoe Lane. This led to her first notable book commission, an event appreciated all the more because it was a story she had liked as a child—*Diamonds and Toads*. This slim paper-bound volume, a popular little tale pointing to the moral that "cross words are as bad dropped from the mouth as toads and vipers, while gentle words are better than roses and diamonds" was printed by Kronheim and destined to number in Aunt Louisa's London Toy Book Series under the imprint of Frederick Warne and Company. Kate talked her younger sister, Fanny, into posing for her as the heroine. No one would know these illustrations were Greenaways unless told.

That same year, 1871, and from the same source, another of those "two-a-penny" fairy tales Kate loved as a little girl came her way to be illustrated anew. This was *Bluebeard*. Kronheim was packaging a set of nine fairy stories, all the work of Madame la Comtesse d'Aulnoy, for the Edinburgh publishers, Gall & Inglis, and Kate Greenaway was told she could illustrate the entire set if she wanted to undertake this sizeable job at the going rate. She did want to, even though her name again would not appear as illustrator and the fee for the nine tales, plus *Diamonds and Toads* would earn her a modest thirty-six pounds. Besides *Bluebeard*, the d'Aulnoy set included *Babes in the Wood, Red Riding Hood, Puss in Boots,* and five other familiar stories translated from Mme. la Comtesse's late eighteenth-century French.

It was partly the result of her father's contacts, as an engraver to printers and publishers, that Kate Greenaway broke into the pages of *Little Folks*. Many of the numerous illustrations she made for this popular magazine between 1873 and 1879 (including the serialization of "Poor Nelly," by Bonavia Hunt) bear the joint signature of daughter and father: "K. Greenaway del." and "J. Greenaway Sc."

Christmas and New Year cards published about 1878.

It was also indirectly through her father, but again entirely on her own merits, that she became a contributor to the *Illustrated London News*—a historic event for her, considering that she had been such an avid follower of the magazine since first she could remember. In the December 26, 1874, issue there is a charming full-page picture of her vision of "A Christmas Dream." She was to contribute similar drawings to every other Christmas issue of the magazine until 1885.

Another milestone was reached in 1874 when she saw her name printed on the title page of a book for the very first time. It was a small volume of fairy stories entitled *Fairy Gifts* or *A Wallet of Wonders,* containing texts by Kathleen Knox and eleven illustrations by her which her father had engraved. That busy year John Greenaway also engraved the drawing Kate had done for *Cassell's Magazine.*

Meanwhile the market for her paintings at The Dudley Gallery had grown. So had the prices. An increasingly fashionable clientele—eventually to include ladies and gentlemen of title—was now being called upon to part with twenty guineas for a charming Greenaway watercolour instead of fifteen. Besides being seen at Dudley's, Kate Greenaway was represented at The Royal Manchester Institution in 1873, also at the Royal Society of British Artists (Suffolk Street Galleries) in 1870, and again there in 1872 and for four successive years thereafter.

Business in general had been good enough for Kate, proudly, to contribute to the purchase, with her father, of the lease of a house in Pemberton Gardens, Holloway. The family moved there from Islington sometime between 1873 and 1874. Although she retained a studio in Islington, Pemberton Gardens was to remain Kate Greenaway's residence until 1885, when, still at the height

(Courtesy The Victoria and Albert Museum, London)

of her fame and with her pictures and rhymes on *Marigold Garden* just completed, she moved into the modern house that Richard Norman Shaw, the architect of New Scotland Yard, had designed for her at Frognal, Hampstead. There she lived out the rest of her years. Her house with its impressive studio still stands, but it is now divided into apartments.

In 1876 Kate Greenaway's earnings amounted to approximately two hundred pounds. In 1877, after she added *St. Nicholas, Scribner's Illustrated Magazine for Boys and Girls,* and the newly established *Graphic* magazine to her markets, and excitedly found herself represented for

Home-Beauty.

"*MINE be a cot*," *for the hours of play,*
   Of the kind that is built by Miss Greenaway,
Where the walls are low, and the roofs are red,
And the birds are gay in the blue o'erhead;
And the dear little figures, in frocks and frills,
Go roaming about at their own sweet wills,
And play with the pups, and reprove the calves,
And do nought in the world (but Work) by halves,
From "Hunt the Slipper" and "Riddle-me-ree"
To watching the cat in the apple-tree.

O Art of the Household! Men may prate
Of their ways "intense" and Italianate,—
They may soar on their wings of sense, and float
To the au delà and the dim remote,—
Till the last sun sink in the last-lit West,
'Tis the Art at the Door that will please the best;
To the end of Time 'twill be still the same,
For the Earth first laughed when the children came!

Austin Dobson.

the first time in The Royal Academy (where her entry, "Musings," sold for twenty guineas), her total annual income came to three hundred pounds. This was about one quarter of what her earnings were to be in the years when royalties from *Under the Window* and her second success, *Kate Greenaway's Birthday Book for Children*, came in. The first printing of the latter, including the French and German editions, was 150,000, a phenomenally large quantity, particularly in those days.

Valentine cards. (Courtesy The Victoria and Albert Museum, London)

OPPOSITE: Kate Greenaway cooperated with the poet Austin Dobson in producing this feature for *The Magazine of Art* in 1883.

Kate Greenaway's greatest luck came in the shape of a gentleman named Edmund Evans, an excellent engraver and printer, and an astute businessman besides. As he was in the printing business, it is not surprising to find that Mr. Evans was an old acquaintance of her father, a contact that had sent Kate hying down to Witley one day in 1877 "with a collection of about fifty drawings she had made," Evans said, "with quaint verses written to them."

The originality of the drawings and the ideas of the verse immediately appealed to Edmund Evans, and there and then he purchased the entire collection with a view to printing them in book form. He saw how this would be a very nice way of keeping both his wood-engraving shop and his printing plant occupied during some slack period ahead. Furthermore, Kate Greenaway's talent looked to him to be on a par with that of Walter Crane and Randolph Caldecott, from the production of whose books he had already greatly profited. The gamble he was taking was, indeed, safe.

After the title of the book was chosen—from the first line of the first verse—printing schedules for *Under the Window* were worked out so that the book would be available in plenty of time for Christmas 1878. No sooner had copies reached the bookshops and been enthusiastically placed on display than a storm of delight swept through the land.

"After I had engraved the blocks and colour blocks," said Evans, "I printed the first edition of twenty thousand copies and was ridiculed by the publishers for risking such a large edition of a six-shilling book, but the edition sold before I could reprint another. . . ." The reprints have continued to this day.

Edmund Evans and Kate Greenaway each had made a fair deal for themselves, evenly dividing the profits on the sales of the book once Evans had recovered his manufacturing costs. The arrangement held on all subsequent ventures. It was a happy and profitable business partnership that, even excluding the *Almanack*, took them through no less than sixteen books, from the first epoch-making venture, *Under the Window* in 1878, through to *The Royal Progress of King Pepito*, published in 1889, twelve years before the undisputed queen of nursery books died.

Book-plate design for Lady
Victoria Herbert.

Christmas card. (In the Frederick Warne Collection)

32

ABOVE AND RIGHT: Two from
a set of twelve illustrations for
"Christmas in Little People-
ton Manor," featured in the
Illustrated London News
(1879).

"No one could draw roses better than Kate Greenaway,"
said Helen Allingham. This
example is from *Under the
Window.*

Little baby, if I threw
This fair blossom down to you,
Would you catch it as you stand,
Holding up each tiny hand,
Looking out of those grey eyes,
Where such deep, deep wonder lies?

KC

Under the window is my garden,
  Where sweet, sweet flowers grow;
And in the pear-tree dwells a robin.
  The dearest bird I know.

UNDER THE WINDOW

ery many thanks for your very pretty and charming book," wrote H. Stacy Marks to Kate Greenaway on October 22, 1878. The noted painter, who had first met and encouraged her in 1871 and had continued to offer artistic advice ever since, was unusually flattering. "So many designs are delightful," he said, "it seems hard to select any special one, but I think . . . the girls with the shuttlecocks [page 45] bear the palm." And: "Did you write the verses also? If so, there is another feather for your cap, for I know how difficult it is to write verses for children."

Kate Greenaway considered these verses to be little more than rough drafts, yet her engraver and printer, Edmund Evans, and Frederick Locker, whom Evans had asked to "look over things" editorially, found them delightfully spontaneous. George Routledge & Sons, with whom Evans had made an agreement to publish *Under the Window* (having no trade distribution facilities of his own), suffered many a qualm about her literary form, but there is no evidence that any changes in her texts were made. Indeed, there was little chance of it. Almost before anyone knew it, the fast-moving Mr. Evans had set the rhymes in type.

The triumph of *Under the Window* made this publication the major milestone of Kate Greenaway's career. Hitherto she had illustrated other people's ideas; in this book she had illustrated her own, enjoying to the full the "fun and fancy" of her imagination. This freedom resulted in the fresh, highly original style that became her hallmark. So it was that from comparative obscurity the shy, retiring, unassuming Kate Greenaway awoke as if in a fairy tale to find the world at her feet.

Two pages in the following selections (pages 41 and 43) are original to the first edition of *Under the Window* but are not to be found in the sixty-four-page volume Frederick Warne has kept in print since taking the book over from George Routledge in 1900.

Little Fanny wears a hat
  Like her ancient Grannie;
Tommy's hoop was (think of that!)
  Given him by Fanny.

Will you be my little wife,
  If I ask you? Do!
I'll buy you such a Sunday frock,
  A nice umbrella, too.

You see, merry Phillis, that dear little maid,
    Has invited Belinda to tea;
Her nice little garden is shaded by trees,—
    What pleasanter place could there be?

There's a cake full of plums, there are strawberries too,
    And the table is set on the green;
I'm fond of a carpet all daisies and grass,—
    Could a prettier picture be seen?

A blackbird (yes, blackbirds delight in warm weather)
    Is flitting from yonder high spray;
He sees the two little ones talking together,—
    No wonder the blackbird is gay!

"Shall I sing?" says the Lark,
"Shall I bloom?" says the Flower;
"Shall I come?" says the Sun,
"Or shall I?" says the Shower.

Sing your song, pretty Bird,
Roses, bloom for an hour;
Shine on, dearest Sun,
Go away, naughty Shower!

Little Miss Patty and Master Paul
Have found two snails on the garden wall.
"These snails," said Paul, "how slow they walk!—
A great deal slower than we can talk.
Make haste, Mr. Snail, travel quicker, I pray;
In a race with our tongues you'd be beaten to-day."

Poor Dicky's Dead!—The bell we toll,
And lay him in the deep, dark hole.
The sun may shine, the clouds may rain,
But Dick will never pipe again!
His quilt will be as sweet as ours,—
Bright buttercups and cuckoo-flowers.

Beneath the lilies—tall, white garden lilies
  The Princess slept, a charmed sleep alway;
For ever were the fairy bluebells ringing,
  For ever thro' the night and thro' the day.

Ere long a prince came riding in the sunshine,
  A wind just swayed the lilies to and fro;
It woke the Princess, tho' the bluebell music
  Kept ringing, ringing, sleepily and low.

School is over,
Oh, what fun!
Lessons finished,—
Play begun.
Who'll run fastest,
You or I?
Who'll laugh loudest?—
Let us try.

K.C.

This little fat Goblin,
  A notable sinner,
Stole cabbages daily,
  For breakfast and dinner.

The Farmer looked sorry;
  He cried, and with pain,
"That rogue has been here
  For his cabbage again!"

That little plump Goblin,
  He laughed, "Ho! ho! ha!
Before me he catches,
  He'll have to run far."

That little fat Goblin,
  He never need sorrow;
He stole three to-day,
  And he'll steal more to-morrow.

43

The boat sails away, like a bird on the wing,
And the little boys dance on the sands in a ring.
The wind may fall, or the wind may rise,—
You are foolish to go; you will stay if you're wise.
The little boys dance, and the little girls run:
If it's bad to have money, it's worse to have none.

KG

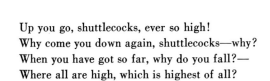

Up you go, shuttlecocks, ever so high!
Why come you down again, shuttlecocks—why?
When you have got so far, why do you fall?—
Where all are high, which is highest of all?

K.G

KATE GREENAWAY'S BIRTHDAY BOOK
FOR CHILDREN

With Verses by Mrs. Sale Barker

ood Evans!" a perfectly respectable newspaper editor punned as his approving eye scanned the second Greenaway book Edmund Evans had engraved. "A most dainty little work," said *Punch* magazine, and "a selling success," exclaimed a delighted Miss Greenaway, who was "looking forward with rejoicing to future pounds and pennies." Never having had many of these to play with, Kate now found them to be "uncommonly nice possessions."

But even in those days success had its irritations. "I really feel quite cross," she wrote to Frederick Locker in 1880, "as I look at the shop windows and see the imitation books. It feels so queer, somehow, to see your ideas taken by someone else and put forth as theirs."

On the brighter side in 1880, besides the prospect of good royalties and better book and magazine commissions, was the satisfaction of seeing another of her watercolours hung in The Royal Academy. It was the fourth time she had been so honoured in as many years.

The *Birthday Book*, originally published in 1880 and still reprinted, contains 350 tiny black-and-white illustrations and twelve illustrations in colour. In addition are Mrs. Barker's verses and, month by month, the pages of ruled lines on which to enter friends' birthdays.

JANUARY

What is he doing, this little Jack Horner;
  There on his three-legged stool?
Is he doing his lessons, or eating his dinner;
  Or merely just playing the fool?

FEBRUARY

Selina Amelia called out to her cat,—
"Oh, Pussy, dear Pussy, I wish you'd grow fat;
Here's a saucer of milk, mixed with oil from the cod,
I hope you won't think that the mixture is odd."

46

MARCH

Dear little maid!—Is she sleeping,
  Or crying her woes to the ground?
Grief, and rest, and a little joy,—
  It is thus the world goes round.

APRIL

Look at this boy as you pass by;
Look, how he's laughing! I'll tell you why:
He made an old woman an April fool:
With vulgar boys that is the rule.

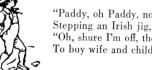

MAY

"Paddy, oh Paddy, now where do you go,
Stepping an Irish jig, dancing just so?"
"Oh, shure I'm off, then, to Dublin town.
To buy wife and children aich a new gown."

JUNE

This girl is walking to London town,
  Her luncheon in her basket;
She's walking, walking up and down,
  Her way—she'll have to ask it.

JULY

Tilly Toddles knocked her head
  A very hard, hard blow;
She loudly cried, and sadly sighed
  "Oh dear! it hurts me so!"

AUGUST

This lady has come to pay a call,
  To have a little chat;
She talks of the weather, she talks of the news,
  She talks of this and of that.

Apparently this little volume prompted Robert Louis Stevenson to write his *Child's Garden of Verses.* According to Graham Balfour, "Louis took the *Birthday Book* up one day, and saying, 'These are rather nice rhymes, and I don't think they would be very difficult to do,' proceeded to try his hand."

SEPTEMBER

Baby ran to meet me, she had a sash all blue,,
    A bran-new gown,
    Just come from town,
    A cap so crisp and new.

OCTOBER

Janet didn't know her lesson,
    Janet said it badly,
    Janet was rebuked severely,
    Janet took it sadly.

NOVEMBER

A brigand's hat! well, what of that
    If there's no head within?
To take off one without the other,
    I really call a sin.

DECEMBER

Christmas! Hear the joy-bells ringing,
Glad hymns in the churches singing;
Of His mercy, of His power,
And the gifts good angels shower!

A DAY IN A CHILD'S LIFE

With Music by Myles B. Foster

This celebration of children in music and pictures is one of Kate Greenaway's loveliest works, a strong secondary motif of flowers flowing through it from the first of its thirty colour pages to the last.

Her intense love of gardens developed during her childhood visits to Nottinghamshire. At the farmhouse belonging to a neighbour of her great-aunt in Rolleston was, she remembered, "my loved one of all the gardens I have ever known." The Fryers grew "the biggest and brightest convolvuluses" . . . and "across the gravel path roses, pinks, stocks, sweet Sultans, the brown scabius, white lilies, red fuchsias," as well as "monster tulips, double white narcissus, peonies, crown imperials, and wallflowers." Some of these flowers, and others, such as daffodils, fox-decorate these pages and, in different form, the pages of *Language of Flowers*, which became her major project in 1884.

Not all the critics were kind to *A Day in a Child's Life*. In 1881, the year it came out, *The Times* of London complained: "Kate Greenaway seems to be lapsing into a rather lackadaisical prettiness of style." Others disagreed, some violently, even to the point of comparing her work to that of the great Botticelli and her flowers to those Van Huysam painted in his meticulous still lifes.

From Paris that year came word that Alexandre Dumas fils had just bought one of her pictures. This delighted Kate immensely.

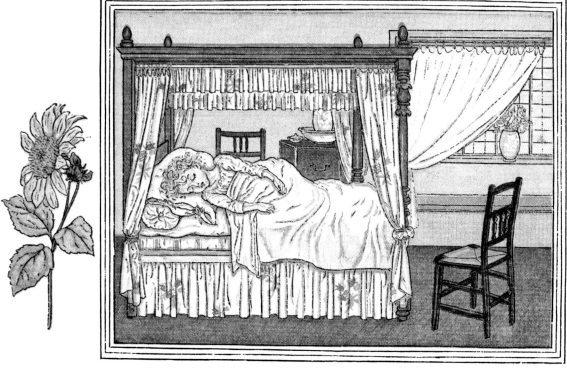

No. 1.

WAKING

Brightly.

1. Wake up! the sun is shi-ning Up-on the win-dow-pane, And hark! the noi-sy spar-rows Are wide a-wake a-gain; Each lit-tle bud and blos-som Has lift-ed up its head To

greet the pleasant sunshine, While you are still in bed!

The sun himself has risen
  To call them, long ago;
And he has tried to wake you
  This last half-hour, you know.

The merry little sunbeams
  Have travelled—oh, so far!
Have crept between the shutters,
  In spite of bolt and bar.

'Twas time, indeed, to wake you,
  At last they seemed to think;
And shot their golden arrows
  Through every hole and chink.

And when the door was opened,
  And Mary came at last,
Your eyes were almost blinded,
  They fell so thick and fast.

Then wake, and, like the flowers,
  Lift up each sleepy head;
It is too bright a morning
  To waste it all in bed.

53

No. 6.

A ROMP

No. 9.

SLEEPING

1. Lul-la-by, lul-la-by, ba - by dear, Take thy rest with-out a fear;
2. Lul-la-by, lul-la-by, gone is the light, Yet let not darkness my ba - by fright,
3. *pp* May thy small dreams no ill things see, Kind heaven keep watch, my babe, o'er thee,

Qui - et sleep, for mo-ther is here,..... E - ver wake-ful e - ver near,
Mo - ther is with her a - mid the night ;.... Then soft-ly sleep, my heart's de-light,
Kind an - gels bright thy guard-ians be,........ And give thee, smil-ing, to day and to me,

E - ver wake - ful,   e - ver near.   Lul - la - by,   lul - la - by!
Then soft - ly   sleep,   my   heart's de - light.   Lul - la - by   lul - la - by!
And give thee, smil - ing,   to   day and to   me.   Lul - la - by,   lul - la - by!

Little Bo-peep has lost her sheep,
And can't tell where to find them;
Leave them alone, and they'll come home,
And bring their tails behind them.

Hark! hark! the dogs bark,
The beggars are coming to town;
Some in rags and some in tags,
And some in a silken gown.
Some gave them white bread,
And some gave them brown,
And some gave them a good horse-whip,
And sent them out of the town.

To market, to market, to buy a plum cake,
Home again, home again, market is late;
To market, to market, to buy a plum bun,
Home again, home again, market is done.

MOTHER GOOSE

or The Old Nursery Rhymes

ccasionally Stacy Marks vied with his friend and kindred critical spirit, John Ruskin, in giving Kate Greenaway the "maximum" benefit of his advice. This usually meant pointing out this or that fault, mostly in relation to her rendering of anatomy, perspective, or what he once singled out as a "naïve defiance of all rules of composition!"

After *Under the Window* became a best seller, he had written: "Don't let *any* success or praise make you puffed up or conceited." Then in another letter: "I am not going to be 'severe' but I *must* ask you not to repeat those funny little black shadows under the feet of your figures—looking in some places like spurs, in others like tadpoles, in others like short stilts."

And now in 1881, after receiving his free copy of *Mother Goose*, he wrote: "You have got rid of the spur-like shadows, but *where*, even in England do you see cabbagy trees?" (as on page 58). And of the Pippin Hill illustration on page 62, "the action of the figure . . . is impossible coming downhill—how about the center of gravity, Madam?" Following further comments of this nature, he concludes, "I don't apologise for telling you the truth from my point of view, because I know you are strong enough to bear it and amiable enough to like it."

Fate plays such funny tricks. Were technique everything, then possibly the work of Miss Greenaway would have been forgotten while that of the meticulous H. Stacy Marks, R.A., would have endured. But it wasn't like that; it was the other way round.

Kate Greenaway's *Mother Goose*, with its forty-eight pages of picture and rhymes, was first published in 1881, the same year as *A Day in a Child's Life*. It was also in 1881 that *Punch* chose to feature Miss Greenaway in the magazine on three occasions. This honour, unprecedented for an illustrator of children's books, was an acknowledgement of her renown and the high regard in which the public now held her.

Mary, Mary, quite contrary,
How does your garden grow?
With silver bells, and cockle shells,
And cowslips all of a row.

Polly put the kettle on,
Polly put the kettle on,
Polly put the kettle on,
We'll all have tea.
Sukey take it off again,
Sukey take it off again,
Sukey take it off again,
They're all gone away.

Cross Patch, lift the latch,
Sit by the fire and spin;
Take a cup, and drink it up,
Then call your neighbours in.

Draw a pail of water,
For my lady's daughter;
My father's a king, and my mother's a queen,
My two little sisters are dressed in green,
Stamping grass and parsley,
Marigold leaves and daisies.
One rush! two rush!
Pray thee, fine lady, come under my bush.

Goosey, goosey, gander,
Where shall I wander?
Up stairs, down stairs,
And in my lady's chamber:
There I met an old man,
Who would not say his prayers;
Take him by the left leg,
Throw him down the stairs.

Tom, Tom, the piper's son,
He learnt to play when he was young,
He with his pipe made such a noise,
That he pleased all the girls and boys.

Daffy-down-dilly has come up to town,
In a yellow petticoat and a green gown.

Diddlty, diddlty, dumpty,
The cat run up the plum tree;
Give her a plum, and down she'll come,
Diddlty, diddlty, dumpty.

Little Tommy Tittlemouse,
Lived in a little house;
He caught fishes
In other men's ditches.

Elsie Marley has grown so fine,
She won't get up to serve the swine;
But lies in bed till eight or nine.
And surely she does take her time.

Lucy Locket, lost her pocket,
Kitty Fisher found it;
There was not a penny in it,
But a ribbon round it.

Ride a cock-horse,
To Banbury-cross,
To see little Johnny
Get on a white horse.

Here am I, little jumping Joan,
When nobody's with me,
I'm always alone.

All around the green gravel,
The grass grows so green,
And all the pretty maids are fit to be seen;
Wash them in milk,
Dress them in silk,
And the first to go down shall be married.

Little lad, little lad,
Where wast thou born?
Far off in Lancashire,
Under a thorn;
Where they sup sour milk
From a ram's horn.

Little Tom Tucker,
He sang for his supper.
What did he sing for?
Why, white bread and butter.
How can I cut it without a knife?
How can I marry without a wife?

My mother, and your mother,
Went over the way;
Said my mother, to your mother,
"It's chop-a-nose day."

Georgie Peorgie, pudding and pie,
Kissed the girls and made them cry;
When the girls begin to play,
Georgie Peorgie runs away.

65

LITTLE ANN, AND OTHER POEMS

With Verses by Jane and Ann Taylor

This time, after receiving his usual free copy of the newest Kate Greenaway book, Stacy Marks was more complimentary to Kate than he had been concerning her *Mother Goose*. "I won't allow the year to pass away," he said, "without thanking you for what is, I think, on the whole, I might say entirely your *best* book."

There were certain exceptions to Kate Greenaway's growing lack of enthusiasm for illustrating books others had written. A case in point was *Little Ann*. Christina M. Gee, a Greenaway expert, reminds us that the collected poems by the Taylors "were Kate Greenaway's favourite childhood reading and were deeply felt and enjoyed." And in M. H. Spielmann's opinion, which concurred with Stacy Marks's, this sixty-four-page volume contained "some of the most delightful and spring-like drawings she ever did."

By 1883, after *Little Ann* and the first of her popular little *Almanacks* came out, the Greenaway rage was reaching its height. Imitators were manifold; fashionable children wore Greenaway clothes, and dolls were prettily dressed to match. In time even statuettes, candelabra, and designs on plates, tiles, and vases were closely copied from characters in her books by various manufacturers in England and on the Continent, particularly in Belgium. A great deal of this "lifting" was done without her prior knowledge and without profit to her except world fame. Even then many of the imitations were poorly done. She was delighted, however, in 1893 when the *Almanack* drawings she had sold turned out beautifully in a wallpaper design.

The original watercolours for *Little Ann*, along with a selection from other books of hers, were sent on exhibition to Paris in 1889. The popularity of Kate Greenaway in France had interested Frederick Locker enough for him to write in 1882: "It has occurred to me that you are about the *only* English artist who has ever been the fashion in France. Bonington and Constable are appreciated, but not more than appreciated. I think anyone writing about you should notice this important fact."

A TRUE STORY

Little Ann and her mother were walking one day
  Through London's wide city so fair,
And business obliged them to go by the way
  That led them through Cavendish Square.

And as they pass'd by the great house of a Lord,
  A beautiful chariot there came,
To take some most elegant ladies abroad,
  Who straightway got into the same.

The ladies in feathers and jewels were seen,
  The chariot was painted all o'er,
The footmen behind were in silver and green,
  The horses were prancing before.

Little Ann by her mother walk'd silent and sad,
  A tear trickled down from her eye,
Till her mother said, "Ann, I should be very glad
  To know what it is makes you cry."

"Mamma," said the child, "see that carriage so fair,
  All cover'd with varnish and gold,
Those ladies are riding so charmingly there
  While we have to walk in the cold.

"You say God is kind to the folks that are good,
  But surely it cannot be true;
Or else I am certain almost, that He would
  Give such a fine carriage to you."

"Look there, little girl," said her mother, "and see
  What stands at that very coach door;
A poor ragged beggar, and listen how she
  A halfpenny tries to implore.

'Dear ladies,' she cries, and the tears trickle down,
  'Relieve a poor beggar, I pray;
I've wander'd all hungry about this wide town,
  And not ate a morsel to-day.

'My father and mother are long ago dead,
  My brother sails over the sea,
And I've scarcely a rag, or a morsel of bread,
  As plainly, I'm sure, you may see . . .

'Some will not attend to my pitiful call,
  Some think me a vagabond cheat;
And scarcely a creature relieves me, of all
  The thousands that traverse the street.

'Then ladies, dear ladies, your pity bestow';—
  Just then a tall footman came round,
And asking the ladies which way they would go,
  The chariot turn'd off with a bound.

"Ah! see, little girl," then her mother replied,
  "How foolish those murmurs have been;
You have but to look on the contrary side,
  To learn both your folly and sin . . .

"Your house and its comforts, you food and your friends,
  'Tis favour in God to confer,
Have you any claim to the bounty He sends,
  Who makes you to differ from her?"

THE GAUDY FLOWER

Alas! that form, and brilliant fire,
  Will never win beholder's love;
It may, indeed, make fools admire,
  But ne'er the wise and good can move.

So grows the tulip, gay and bold,
  The broadest sunshine its delight;
Like rubies, or like burnish'd gold,
  It shows its petals, glossy bright.

But who the gaudy floweret crops,
  As if to court a sweet perfume!
Admired it blows, neglected drops,
  And sinks unheeded to its doom.

The virtues of the heart may move
  Affections of a genial kind;
While beauty fails to stir our love,
  And wins the eye, but not the mind.

Why does my Anna toss her head,
  And look so scornfully around,
As if she scarcely deign'd to tread
  Upon the daisy-dappled ground?

Does fancied beauty fire thine eye,
  The brilliant tint, the satin skin?
Does the loved glass, in passing by,
  Reflect a graceful form and thin?

THE BUTTERFLY

The Butterfly, an idle thing,
Nor honey makes, nor yet can sing,
   As do the bee and bird;
Nor does it, like the prudent ant,
Lay up the grain for times of want,
   A wise and cautious hoard.

My youth is but a summer's day:
Then like the bee and ant I'll lay
   A store of learning by;
And though from flower to flower I rove,
My stock of wisdom I'll improve
   Nor be a butterfly.

DIRTY JIM

There was one little Jim,
'Tis reported of him.
   And must be to his lasting disgrace,
That he never was seen
With hands at all clean,
   Nor yet ever clean was his face.

His friends were much hurt
To see so much dirt,
   And often they made him quite clean;
But all was in vain,
He got dirty again,
   And not at all fit to be seen.

It gave him no pain
To hear them complain,
   Nor his own dirty clothes to survey;
His indolent mind
No pleasure could find
   In tidy and wholesome array.

The idle and bad,
Like this little lad,
   May love dirty ways, to be sure;
But good boys are seen
To be decent and clean,
   Although they are ever so poor.

THE SPIDER

"Oh, look at that great ugly spider!" said Ann;
And screaming, she brush'd it away with her fan;
" 'Tis a frightful black creature as ever can be,
I wish that it would not come crawling on me."

"Indeed," said mother, "I'll venture to say,
The poor thing will try to keep out of your way;
For after the fright, and the fall, and the pain,
It has much more occasion than you to complain.

"But why should you dread the poor insect, my dear?
If it *hurt* you, there'd be some excuse for your fear;
But its little black legs, as it hurried away,
Did but tickle your arm, as they went, I dare say.

"For *them* to fear *us* we must grant to be just,
Who in less than a moment can tread them to dust;
But certainly *we* have no cause for alarm;
For, were they to try, they could do us no harm.

"Now look! it has got to its home; do you see
What a delicate web it has spun in the tree?
Why here, my dear Ann, is a lesson for you:
Come learn from this spider what patience can do!

"And when at your business you're tempted to play,
Recollect what you see in this insect to-day,
Or else, to your shame, it may seem to be true,
That a poor little spider is wiser than you."

They came to the house, and ask'd at the gate,
  "Is Benjamin Green now at home?"
But Benjamin did not allow them to wait,
  And brought them both into the room.

And he smiled, and he laugh'd, and caper'd with joy,
  His little companions to greet:
"And we too are happy," said each little boy,
  "Our playfellow dear thus to meet."

"Come, walk in our garden, this morning so fine,
  We may, for my father gives leave:
And more, he invites you to stay here and dine:
  And a most happy day we shall have!"

But when in the garden, they found twas the same
  They saw as they walk'd in the road:
And near the high wall when those little boys came,
  They started as if from a toad:

"That large ring of iron, you see on the ground,
  With terrible teeth like a saw,"
Said their friend, "the guard of our garden is found,
  And it keeps all intruders in awe.

THE BOYS AND THE APPLE-TREE

As William and Thomas were walking one day,
  They came by a fine orchard's side:
They would rather eat apples than spell, read, or play,
  And Thomas to William then cried:

"O brother, look yonder! what clusters hang there!
  I'll try and climb over the wall:
I must have an apple; I will have a pear;
  Although it should cost me a fall!"

Said William to Thomas, "To steal is a sin,
  Mamma has oft told this to thee:
I never have stolen, nor will I begin,
  So the apples may hang on the tree."

"You are a good boy, as you ever have been,"
  Said Thomas, "let's walk on, my lad:
We'll call on our schoolfellow, Benjamin Green,
  Who to see us I know will be glad."

"If any the warning without set at naught,
  Their legs then this man-trap must tear":
Said William to Thomas, "So you'd have been caught,
  If you had leapt over just there."

Cried Thomas in terror of what now he saw,
  "With my faults I will heartily grapple;
For I learn what may happen by breaking a law,
  Although but in stealing an apple."

THE CHILD'S MONITOR

The wind blows down the largest tree,
And yet the wind I cannot see!
Playmates far off, who have been kind.
My thought can bring before my mind;
The past by it is present brought,
And yet I cannot see my thought;
The charming rose scents all the air,
Yet I can see no perfume there.
Blithe Robin's notes how sweet, how clear!
From his small bill they reach my ear,
And whilst upon the air they float,
I hear, yet cannot see a note.
When I would do what is forbid,
By *something* in my heart I'm chid;
When good, I think, then quick and pat,
That *something* says, "My child, do that":
When I too near the stream would go,
So pleased to see the waters flow,

That *something* says, without a sound,
"Take care, dear child, you may be drown'd":
And for the poor whene'er I grieve,
That *something* says, "A penny give."

Thus *something* very near must be,
Although invisible to me;
Whate'er I do, it sees me still:
O then, good Spirit, guide my will.

SOPHIA'S FOOL'S-CAP

Sophia was a little child,
Obliging, good, and very mild,
Yet lest of dress she should be vain,
Mamma still dress'd her well, but plain.
Her parents, sensible and kind,
Wish'd only to adorn her mind;
No other dress, when good, had she,
But useful, neat simplicity.

Though seldom, yet when she was rude,
Or ever in a naughty mood,
Her punishment was this disgrace,
A large fine cap, adorn'd with lace,
With feathers and with ribbons too;
The work was neat, the fashion new,
Yet, as a fool's-cap was its name,
She dreaded much to wear the same.

A lady, fashionably gay,
Did to mamma a visit pay:
Sophia stared, then whisp'ring said,
"Why, dear mamma, look at her head!
To be so tall and wicked too,
The strangest thing I ever knew:
What naughty tricks, pray, has she done,
That they have put that fool's-cap on?"

GEORGE AND THE CHIMNEY-SWEEP

His petticoats now George cast off.
  For he was four years old;
His trousers were of nankeen stuff,
  With buttons bright as gold.
"May I," said George, "just go abroad,
  My pretty clothes to show?
May I, mamma? but speak the word";
  The answer was, "No, no."

"Go, run below, George, in the court,
  But go not in the street,
Lest boys with you should make some sport
  Or gypsies you should meet."
Yet, though forbidden, he went out,
  That other boys might spy,
And proudly there he walk'd about,
  And thought—"How fine am I!"

But whilst he strutted through the street,
  With looks both vain and pert,
A sweep-boy pass'd, whom not to meet,
  He slipp'd—into the dirt.
The sooty lad, whose heart was kind,
  To help him quickly ran,
And grasp'd his arm, with—"Never mind,
  You're up, my little man."

Sweep wiped his clothes with labour vain,
  And begg'd him not to cry;
And when he'd blacken'd every stain,
  Said, "Little sir, good-bye."
Poor George, almost as dark as sweep,
  And smear'd in dress and face,
Bemoans with sobs, both loud and deep,
  His well-deserved disgrace.

JAMES AND THE SHOULDER OF MUTTON

Young Jem at noon return'd from school,
  As hungry as could be,
He cried to Sue, the servant-maid,
  "My dinner give to me."

Said Sue, "It is not yet come home;
  Besides, it is not late."
"No matter that," cries little Jem,
  "I do not like to wait."

Quick to the baker's Jemmy went
  And ask'd, "Is dinner done?"
"It is," replied the baker's man.
  "Then home I'll with it run."

"Nay, Sir," replied he prudently,
  "I tell you 'tis too hot,
And much too heavy 'tis for you."
  "I tell you it is not.

"Papa, mamma, are both gone out,
  And I for dinner long;
So give it me, it is all mine,
  And, baker hold your tongue."

Now near the door young Jem was come,
  He round the corner turn'd,
But oh, sad fate! unlucky chance!
  The dish his fingers burn'd.

Now in the kennel down fell dish,
  And down fell all the meat;
Swift went the pudding in the stream,
  And sail'd along the street.

The people laugh'd, and rude boys grinn'd
  At mutton's hapless fall;
But though ashamed, young Jemmy cried,
  "Better lose part than all."

The shoulder by the knuckle seized,
  His hands both grasp'd it fast,
And deaf to all their gibes and cries,
  He gain'd his home at last.

"Impatience is a fault," cries Jem,
  "The baker told me true;
In future I will patient be,
  And mind what says our Sue."

74

NEGLIGENT MARY

Ah, Mary! what, do you for dolly not care?
  And why is she left on the floor?
Forsaken, and cover'd with dust, I declare;
  With you I must trust her no more.

I thought you were pleased, as you took her so gladly,
  When on your birthday she was sent;
Did I ever suppose you would use her so sadly?
  Was that, do you think, what I meant?

With her bonnet of straw you once were delighted,
  And trimm'd it so pretty with pink;
But now it is crumpled, and dolly is slighted:
  Her nurse quite forgets her, I think.

Suppose now—for Mary is *dolly* to me,
  Whom I love to see tidy and fair—
Suppose I should leave you, as dolly I see,
  In tatters, and comfortless there.

But dolly feels nothing, as you do, my dear,
  Nor cares for her negligent nurse:
If I were as careless as you are, I fear,
  Your lot, and my fault, would be worse.

And therefore it is, in my Mary, I strive
  To check every fault that I see:
Mary's doll is but waxen—mamma's is alive,
  And of far more importance than she.

THE GOOD-NATURED GIRLS

Two good little children, named Mary and Ann,
Both happily live, as good girls always can;
And though they are not either sullen or mute,
They seldom or never are heard to dispute.

If one wants a thing that the other would like—
Well,—what do they do? Must they quarrel and strike?
No, each is so willing to give up her own,
That such disagreements are there never known.

LANGUAGE OF FLOWERS

ow John Ruskin had fun telling Kate what he did and didn't like about her newest creation; mostly what he didn't.

"You and your publishers are both and all geese," said he in a letter dated January 15, 1885. "You put as much work in that *Language of Flowers* as would have served three years' book making if you had only drawn boldly, coloured truly and given six for sixty pages. The public will always pay a shilling for a penny's worth of what it likes, it won't pay a penny for a pound's worth of camomile tea. You draw, let me colour next time."

Mercifully Kate Greenaway never gave him the chance. Despite Mr. Ruskin's growls, the book was, as Kate would have termed it, another "selling success." Furthermore, to many collectors, this small-size book with its eighty pages (forty-eight in colour) is the loveliest little Greenaway book of all, the flowers and fruit being pointed to as "the highest point of her art."

Unfortunately, the smallness of the illustrations in the book and the extreme delicacy both of their line and tone make it all but impossible to reproduce the pages satisfactorily in colour without the originals. As in the case of other books, these are no longer together; all her drawings are scattered throughout the world in private collections, libraries, and museums.

Acacia	*Friendship*
Acanthus	*Artifice*
Almond	*Indiscretion*
Aloe	*Grief*
Alyssum (Sweet)	*Worth beyond beauty*
Amaryllis	*Pride*
Ambrosia	*Love returned*
Anemone, Garden	*Forsaken*
Apple	*Temptation*
Ash Tree	*Grandeur*
Aspen Tree	*Lamentation*
Aster, China	*Variety*
Azalea	*Temperance*
Birch	*Meekness*
Bittersweet (Nightshade)	*Truth*
Bluebell	*Constancy*
Bramble	*Lowliness*
Broom	*Humility*
Buttercup (Kingcup)	*Ingratitude*
Cactus	*Warmth*
Camomile	*Energy in adversity*
Carnation, Red	*Alas for my poor heart*
Carnation, Pink	*Woman's love*
Carnation, Striped	*Refusal*
Carnation, Yellow	*Disdain*
Cedar	*Strength*
Chestnut Tree, Horse	*Luxury*
Chicory	*Frugality*
Chrysanthemum, Chinese	*Cheerfulness under adversity*
Chrysanthemum, Red	*I love*

Chrysanthemum, White	*Truth*
Chrysanthemum, Yellow	*Slighted love*
Cinquefoil	*Maternal affection*
Clover, four-leaved	*Be mine*
Cockscomb	*Foppery*
Columbine	*Folly*
Corn	*Riches*
Crocus, Spring	*Youthful gladness*
Cyclamen	*Diffidence*
Cypress	*Mourning*
Daffodil	*Regard*
Dahlia	*Instability*
Daisy	*Innocence*
Daisy, Michaelmas	*Farewell*
Dock	*Patience*
Dogwood	*Durability*
Eglantine	*Poetry*
Elm	*Dignity*
Elm, American	*Patriotism*
Endive	*Frugality*
Fern	*Fascination*
Fir Tree	*Elevation*
Fleur-de-lis	*Flame*
Forget-me-not	*True love*
Foxglove	*Insincerity*
Geranium, Dark	*Melancholy*
Geranium, Ivy	*Bridal favour*
Geranium, Scarlet	*Comforting*
Golden Rod	*Precaution*
Harebell	*Submission*
Heliotrope	*Devotion*
Hemlock	*You will be my death*
Hibiscus	*Delicate beauty*
Holly	*Foresight*
Hollyhock	*Ambition*
Honeysuckle	*Generous and devoted affection*
Hydrangea	*Heartlessness*
Iris	*Message*
Ivy	*Fidelity*
Jasmine	*Amiability*
Judas Tree	*Unbelief*
Lady's Slipper	*Capricious beauty*
Larch	*Audacity*
Larkspur	*Lightness*
Laurel, Mountain	*Ambition*
Lavender	*Distrust*
Lemon	*Zest*
Lichen	*Solitude*
Lilac, Purple	*First emotions of love*
Lilac, White	*Youthful innocence*
Lily, Water	*Purity of heart*
Lily, White	*Purity*
Lily of the Valley	*Return of happiness*
Lime Tree	*Conjugal love*
Linden, American	*Matrimony*
Locust Tree	*Elegance*
London Pride	*Frivolity*
Lotus Flower	*Estranged love*
Lotus Leaf	*Recantation*

78

Lupine	*Imagination*
Magnolia	*Love of nature*
Maple	*Reserve*
Marigold	*Grief*
Mimosa	*Sensitiveness*
Mint	*Virtue*
Mistletoe	*I surmount difficulties*
Morning Glory	*Affection*
Mushroom	*Suspicion*
Myrrh	*Gladness*
Myrtle	*Love*
Narcissus	*Egotism*
Nasturtium	*Patriotism*
Nightshade	*Truth*
Oak Tree	*Hospitality*
Oleander	*Beware*
Olive	*Peace*
Orange Blossoms	*Your purity equals your loveliness*
Orange Tree	*Generosity*
Palm	*Victory*
Pansy	*Thoughts*
Passion Flower	*Religious superstition*
Pea, Sweet	*Departure*
Pear Tree	*Comfort*
Peppermint	*Warmth of feeling*
Periwinkle, Blue	*Early friendship*
Phlox	*Unanimity*
Pine	*Pity*
Pink	*Boldness*
Pink, Mountain	*Aspiring*
Plum Tree	*Fidelity*
Pomegranate	*Foolishness*
Poplar, Black	*Courage*
Poppy, Scarlet	*Fantastic extravagance*
Poppy, White	*Sleep*
Primrose	*Early youth*
Quince	*Temptation*
Rhododendron	*Danger*
Rose	*Love*
Rose, Bridal	*Happy love*
Rose, Burgundy	*Unconscious beauty*
Rose, Cabbage	*Ambassador of love*
Rose, Damask	*Brilliant complexion*
Rose, Deep red	*Bashful shame*
Rose, Single	*Simplicity*
Rose, White	*I am worthy of you*
Rose, Yellow	*Jealousy*
Saffron	*Beware of excess*
Sage	*Domestic virtue*
St. John's Wort	*Superstition*
Scabius	*Unfortunate love*
Shamrock	*Lightheartedness*
Snakesfoot	*Horror*
Snapdragon	*Presumption*
Snowdrop	*Hope*
Sorrel	*Affection*
Spearmint	*Warmth of sentiment*
Stock	*Lasting beauty*
Sunflower, Dwarf	*Adoration*

79

Sunflower, Tall	*Haughtiness*
Sweetbrier, American	*Simplicity*
Sweet pea	*Delicate pleasures*
Sweet William	*Gallantry*
Sycamore	*Curiosity*
Syringa	*Memory*
Tansy, wild	*I declare war against you*
Teasel	*Misanthropy*
Thyme	*Activity*
Trefoil	*Revenge*
Trumpet Flower	*Fame*
Tuberose	*Dangerous pleasures*
Tulip, Red	*Declaration of love*
Tulip, Yellow	*Hopeless love*
Vervain	*Enchantment*
Violet, Sweet	*Modesty*
Walnut	*Intellect*
Wallflower	*Fidelity in adversity*
Willow, Weeping	*Mourning*
Witch Hazel	*A spell*
Wormwood	*Absence*
Xanthiym	*Rudeness*
Xeranthemum	*Rudeness*
Yew	*Sorrow*
Zinnia	*Thoughtfulness about friends*

DAFFODILS

I wandered lonely as a cloud
   That floats on high o'er vales and hills,
When all at once I saw a crowd,
   A host of golden Daffodils;
Beside the lake, beneath the trees,
Fluttering and dancing in the breeze.

Continuous as the stars that shine
   And twinkle in the milky way,
They stretched in never-ending line
   Along the margin of a bay:
Ten thousand saw I at a glance,
Tossing their heads in sprightly dance.

The waves beside them danced; but they
   Outdid the sparkling waves in glee;
A poet could not but be gay,
   In such a jocund company;
I gazed and gazed, but little thought
What wealth to me the show had brought!

For oft when on my couch I lie,
   In vacant or in pensive mood,
They flash upon that inward eye
   Which is the bliss of solitude;
And then my heart with pleasure fills,
And dances with the Daffodils.

WORDSWORTH

THE SENSITIVE PLANT

A Sensitive Plant in a garden grew,
And the young winds fed it with silver dew,
And it opened its fan-like leaves to the light,
And closed them beneath the kisses of Night.

But none ever trembled and panted with bliss
In the garden, the field, or the wilderness,
Like doe in the noontide with love's sweet want,
As the companionless Sensitive Plant.

The snowdrop, and then the violet,
Arose from the ground with warm rain wet,
And their breath was mixed with fresh odour, sent,
From the turf, like the voice and the instrument.

Then the pied wind-flowers and the tulip tall,
And narcissi, the fairest among them all,
Who gaze on their eyes in the stream's recess,
Till they die of their own dear loveliness.

And the naiad-like lily of the vale,
Whom youth makes so fair and passion so pale,
That the light of its tremulous bells is seen
Through their pavilions of tender green;

And the hyacinth purple, and white, and blue,
Which flung from its bells a sweet peal anew
Of music so delicate, soft and intense,
It was felt like an odour within the sense!

And the rose like a nymph to the bath addrest,
Which unveiled the depth of her glowing breast,
Till, fold after fold, to the fainting air
The soul of her beauty and love lay bare.

And the wand-like lily, which lifted up,
As a Mænad, its moonlight-coloured cup,
Till the fiery star, which is its eye,
Gazed through the clear dew on the tender sky;

And the jessamine faint, and the sweet tuberose,
The sweetest flower for scent that blows;
And all rare blossoms from every clime
Grew in that garden in perfect prime.

The Sensitive Plant, which could give small fruit
Of the love which it felt from the leaf to the root,
Received more than all [flowers], it loved more than ever,
Where none wanted but it, could belong to the giver—

For the Sensitive Plant has no bright flower:
Radiance and odour are not its dower;
It loves, even like Love its deep heart is full,
It desires what it has not, the beautiful!

Each and all like ministering angels were
For the Sensitive Plant sweet joy to bear,
Whilst the lagging hours of the day went by
Like windless clouds o'er a tender sky.

And when evening descended from heaven above,
And the earth was all rest, and the air was all love,
And delight, though less bright, was far more deep,
And the day's veil fell from the world of sleep,

The Sensitive Plant was the earliest
Up-gathered into the bosom of rest:
A sweet child weary of its delight,
The feeblest, and yet the favourite,
Cradled within the embrace of night.

SHELLEY

MARIGOLD GARDEN

Kate Greenaway's wonderful skill in the use of costumes was no free gift from the gods, not just a flair for costume," wrote Austin Dobson. "Like her skill in drawing it was the result of years and years of loving study, of meticulous labour and attention to detail."

In spirit and design *Marigold Garden*, said to have been the author's favourite book, cames closer to *Under the Window* than anything else she did. *Marigold Garden*, completed seven years after that first triumph, shows her increased stature as an artist in the surer drawing, greater attention to detail, also in her more subtle use of colour noticeable throughout the sixty-four pages.

In 1885 K. G., as Kate's intimate friends called her, was at the pinnacle of her success. She had just moved into her new house at Frognal with its larger, lighter, and "altogether more practical" studio. She was happy, too, with her increasing popularity in America. This was such that the publishers initially shipped more copies of *Marigold Garden* to New York than they reserved for English sales. America also took twice the quantity that England did of her *Almanack* that year. It was a trend that was to continue with subsequent books.

In the portrayal of childhood, no artist of her day, perhaps none of any day, could combine charm, beauty, and gentleness with such style as Kate Greenaway. "The Cats Have Come to Tea," the original watercolour of which resides in the Royal Library at Windsor Castle, is but one lovely example.

THE CATS

HAVE COME TO TEA

What did she see—oh, what did she see,
As she stood leaning against the tree?
Why all the cats had come to tea.

What a fine turn out—from round about,
All the houses had let them out,
And here they were with scamper and shout.

"Mew—mew—mew!" was all they could say,
And, "We hope we find you well to-day."

Oh, what should she do—oh, what should she do?
What a lot of milk they would get through;
For here they were with "Mew—mew—mew!"

She didn't know—oh, she didn't know,
If bread and butter they'd like or no;
They might want little mice, oh! oh! oh!

Dear me—oh, dear me,
All the cats had come to tea.

THE CATS HAVE COME TO TEA.

TO MYSTERY LAND

Oh, dear, how will it end?
Peggy and Susie how naughty
  you are.
You little know where you are,
Going so far, and so high,
Nearly up to the sky.
Perhaps it's a Giant who
  lives there,
And perhaps it's a lovely
  Princess.
But you very well know
You've no business to go;
You'll get yourselves into a mess.

Oh, dear, I'm sure it is true;
Whatever on earth can it matter
  to you?
For you know it—oh, fie—
That it's naughty to pry
Into others' affairs—
Into other folks' houses to go,
Where you know
You're not asked.
So you'd better come back
While there's time, it is plain.
Go home—and be never
So naughty again.

UNDER ROSE ARCHES

Under Rose Arches to Rose Town—
  Rose Town on the top of the hill;
For the Summer wind blows and music goes,
  And the violins sound shrill.

Oh, Roses shall be for her carpet,
  And her curtains of Roses so fair;
And a Rosy crown, while far adown
  Floats her long golden hair.

Twist and twine Roses and Lilies,
  And little leaves green,
  Fit for a queen;
Twist and twine Roses and Lilies.

Twist and twine Roses and Lilies,
  And all the bells ring,
  And all the people sing;
Twist and twine Roses and Lilies.

TIP-A-TOE

Tip-a-toe,
See them go;
One, two, three—
Chloe, Prue, and me;
Up and down,
To the town.
A Lord was there,
And the Lady fair.
And what did they sing?
Oh, "Ring-a-ding-ding";
And the Black Crow flew off
With the Lady's Ring.

THE LITTLE QUEEN'S COMING

With Roses—red Roses,
  We'll pelt her with Roses,
And Lilies—white Lilies we'll drop at
  her feet;
The little Queen's coming,
  The people are running—
The people are running to greet and
  to meet.

Then clash out a welcome,
  Let all the bells sound, come,
To give her a welcoming proud and
  sweet.
How her blue eyes will beam,
  And her golden curls gleam,
When the sound of our singing rings
  down the street.

FROM WONDER WORLD

Out of Wonder World I think you
  come,
For in your eyes the wonder comes
  with you.
The stars are the windows of Heaven,
And sometimes I think you peep
  through.
Oh, little girl, tell us do the Flowers
Tell you secrets when they find you
  all alone?
Or the Birds and Butterflies whisper
Of things to us unknown?

Or do angel voices speak to you so softly,
When *we* only hear a little wind sigh;
And the peaceful dew of Heaven fall upon you
When *we* only see a white cloud passing by?

WISHES

Oh, if you were a little boy,
　　And I was a little girl—
Why you would have some whiskers grow
　　And then my hair would curl.

Ah! if I could have whiskers grow,
　　I'd let you have my curls;
But what's the use of wishing it—
　　Boys never can be girls.

THE FOUR PRINCESSES

Four Princesses lived in a Green Tower—
    A Bright Green Tower in the middle of the
       sea;
And no one could think—oh, no one could
      think—
    Who the Four Princesses could be.

One looked to the North, and one to the South,
    And one to the East, and one to the West;
They were all so pretty, so very pretty,
    You could not tell which was the prettiest.

WHEN WE WENT OUT WITH GRANDMAMMA

When we went out with Grandmamma—
  Mamma said for a treat—
Oh, dear, how stiff we had to walk
  As we went down the street.

One on each side we had to go,
  And never laugh or loll;
I carried Prim, her Spaniard dog,
  And Tom—her parasol.

THE QUEEN

OF

THE PIRATE ISLE

By Bret Harte

ith each new Kate Greenaway book there was always someone *besides* her publishers eager to say it was "the best thing" she had ever done. This time John Ruskin told her so. M. H. Spielmann, while disagreeing, explained why. "The drawings are treated in a more natural and less quaint and decorative manner, . . . that is what her mentor [Ruskin] had always been clamouring for." Yet Spielmann could not help but admit that the title page decoration [below] *was* "one of the prettiest vignettes she ever drew."

The story by Bret Harte, the American writer, journalist, and poet, who was a contemporary of Kate Greenaway's, is printed here in full, with a selection of her illustrations, all of which were originally printed in colour by Edmund Evans. The book was published in 1886 and reissued in 1900 by Frederick Warne & Co., who have since kept this classic in print.

I first knew her as the Queen of the Pirate Isle. To the best of my recollection she had no reasonable right to that title. She was only nine years old, inclined to plumpness and good humour, deprecated violence, and had never been to sea. Need it be added that she did *not* live in an island and that her name was "Polly."

Perhaps I ought to explain that she had already known other experiences of a purely imaginative character. Part of her existence had been passed as a Beggar Child—solely indicated by a shawl tightly folded round her shoulders and chills,—as a Schoolmistress, unnecessarily severe; as a Preacher, singularly personal in his remarks, and once, after reading one of Cooper's novels, as an Indian Maiden. This was, I believe, the only instance when she had borrowed from another's fiction. Most of the characters that she assumed for days and sometimes weeks at a time were purely original in conception; some so much so as to be vague to the general understanding. I remember that her personation of a certain Mrs. Smith, whose individuality was supposed to be sufficiently represented by a sun-bonnet worn wrongside before and a weekly addition to her family, was never perfectly appreciated by her own circle although she lived the character for a month. Another creation known as "The Proud Lady"—a being whose excessive and unreasonable haughtiness was so pronounced as to give her features the expression of extreme nausea—caused her mother so much alarm that it had to be abandoned. This was easily effected. The Proud Lady was understood to have died. Indeed, most of Polly's impersonations were got rid of in this way, although it by no means prevented their subsequent reappearance. "I thought Mrs. Smith was dead," remonstrated her mother at the posthumous appearance of that lady with a new infant. "She was buried alive and kem to!" said Polly with a melancholy air. Fortunately, the representation of a resuscitated person required such extraordinary acting, and was, through some uncertainty of conception, so closely allied in facial expression to the Proud Lady, that Mrs. Smith was resuscitated only for a day.

The origin of the title of the Queen of the Pirate Isle, may be briefly stated as follows:

An hour after luncheon, one day, Polly, Hickory Hunt, her cousin, and Wan Lee, a Chinese page, were crossing the nursery floor in a Chinese junk. The sea was calm and the sky cloudless. Any change in the weather was as unexpected as it is in books. Suddenly a West Indian Hurricane, purely local in character and unfelt anywhere else, struck Master Hickory and threw him overboard, whence, wildly swimming for his life and carrying Polly on his back, he eventually reached a Desert Island in the closet. Here the rescued party put up a tent made of a table cloth providentially snatched from the raging billows, and from two o'clock until four, passed six weeks on the island supported only by a piece of candle, a box of matches, and two peppermint lozenges. It was at this time that it became necessary to account for Polly's existence among them, and this was only effected by an alarming sacrifice of their morality; Hickory and Wan Lee instantly became *Pirates*, and at once elected Polly as their Queen. The royal duties, which seemed to be purely maternal, consisted in putting the Pirates to bed after a day of rapine and bloodshed, and in feeding them with liquorice water through a quill in a small bottle. Limited as her functions were, Polly performed them with inimitable gravity and unquestioned sincerity. Even when her companions sometimes hesitated from actual hunger or fatigue and forgot their guilty part, she never faltered. It was her *real* existence—her other life of being washed, dressed, and put to bed at certain hours by her mother was the *illusion*.

Doubt and scepticism came at last,—and came from Wan Lee! Wan Lee of all creatures! Wan Lee, whose silent, stolid, mechanical performance of a Pirate's duties—a perfect imitation like all his household work—had been their one delight and fascination!

It was just after the exciting capture of a merchantman with the indiscriminate slaughter of all on board—a spectacle on which the round blue eyes of the plump Polly had gazed with royal and maternal tolerance, and they were burying the booty—two table spoons and a thimble in the corner of the closet—when Wan Lee stolidly rose.

93

"Melican boy pleenty foolee! Melican boy no Pilat!" said the little Chinaman, substituting "l's" for "r's" after his usual fashion.

"Wotcher say?" said Hickory, reddening with sudden confusion.

"Melican boy's papa heap lickee him—spose him leal Pilat," continued Wan Lee, doggedly. "Melican boy Pilat *inside* housee; Chinee boy Pilat *outside* housee. First chop Pilat."

Staggered by this humiliating statement, Hickory recovered himself in character. "Ah! Ho!" he shrieked, dancing wildly on one leg, "Mutiny and Splordinashun! Way with him to the yard arm."

"Yald alm—heap foolee! Allee same clothes hoss for washee washee."

It was here necessary for the Pirate Queen to assert her authority, which, as I have before stated was somewhat confusingly maternal. "Go to bed instantly without your supper," she said, seriously. "Really, I never saw such bad pirates. Say your prayers, and see that you're up early to church tomorrow." It should be explained that in deference to Polly's proficiency as a preacher, and probably as a relief to their uneasy consciences, Divine Service had always been held on the Island. But Wan Lee continued:—

"Me no shabbee Pilat *inside* housee; me shabbee Pilat *outside* housee. Spose you lun away longside Chinee boy—Chinee boy makee you Pilat."

Hickory softly scratched his leg while a broad, bashful smile almost closed his small eyes. "Wot!" he asked.

"Mebbee you too frightend to lun away. Melican boy's papa heap lickee."

This last infamous suggestion fired the corsair's blood. "Dy'ar think we daresent," said Hickory, desperately, but with an uneasy glance at Polly. "I'll show yer to-morrow."

The entrance of Polly's mother at this moment put an end to Polly's authority and dispersed the pirate band, but left Wan Lee's proposal and Hickory's rash acceptance ringing in the ears of the Pirate Queen. That evening she was unusually silent. She would have taken Bridget, her nurse, into her confidence, but this would have involved a long explanation of her own feelings, from which, like all imaginative children, she shrank. She, however, made preparation for the proposed flight by settling in her mind which of her two dolls she would take. A wooden creature with easy going knees and movable hair seemed to be more fit for hard service and any indiscriminate

94

scalping that might turn up hereafter. At supper, she timidly asked a question of Bridget. "Did ye ever hear the loikes uv that, Ma'am?" said the Irish handmaid with affectionate pride. "Shure the darlint's head is filled noight and day with ancient history. She's after asking me now if Queen's ever run away!" To Polly's remorseful confusion here her good father, equally proud of her precocious interest and his own knowledge, at once interfered with an unintelligible account of the abdication of various Queens in history until Polly's head ached again. Well meant as it was, it only settled in the child's mind that she must keep the awful secret to herself and that no one could understand her.

The eventful day dawned without any unusual sign of importance. It was one of the cloudless summer days of the California foot hills, bright, dry, and as the morning advanced, hot in the white sunshine. The actual, prosaic house in which the Pirates apparently lived, was a mile from a mining settlement on a beautiful ridge of pine woods sloping gently towards a valley on the one side, and on the other falling abruptly into a dark deep olive gulf of pine trees, rocks, and patches of red soil. Beautiful as the slope was, looking over to the distant snow peaks which seemed to be in another world than theirs, the children found a greater attraction in the fascinating depths of a mysterious gulf, or "cañon," as it was called, whose very name filled their ears with a weird music. To creep to the edge of the cliff, to sit upon the brown branches of some fallen pine, and putting aside the dried tassels to look down upon the backs of wheeling hawks that seemed to hang in mid-air was a never failing delight. Here Polly would try to trace the winding red ribbon of road that was continually losing itself among the dense pines of the opposite mountains; here she would listen to the far off strokes of a woodman's axe, or the rattle of some heavy waggon, miles

away, crossing the pebbles of a dried up water course. Here, too, the prevailing colours of the mountains, red and white and green, most showed themselves. There were no frowning rocks to depress the children's fancy, but everywhere along the ridge pure white quartz bared itself through the red earth like smiling teeth; the very pebbles they played with were streaked with shining mica like bits of looking-glass. The distance was always green and summer-like, but the colour they most loved, and which was most familiar to them, was the dark red of the ground beneath their

feet everywhere. It showed itself in the roadside bushes; its red dust pervaded the leaves of the overhanging laurel, it coloured their shoes and pinafores; I am afraid it was often seen in Indian-like patches on their faces and hands. That it may have often given a sanguinary tone to their fancies, I have every reason to believe.

It was on this ridge that the three children gathered at ten o'clock that morning. An earlier flight had been impossible on account of Wan Lee being obliged to perform his regular duty of blackening the shoes of Polly and Hickory before breakfast,—a menial act which in the pure Republic of childhood was never thought inconsistent with the loftiest piratical ambition. On the ridge they met one "Patsey," the son of a neighbour, sun burned, broad-brimmed hatted, red handed, like themselves. As there were afterwards some doubts expressed whether he joined the Pirates of his own free will, or was captured by them, I endeavour to give the colloquy exactly as it occurred:—

Patsey. "Hallo, fellers."

The Pirates. "Hello!"

Patsey. "Goin' to hunt bars? Dad seed a lot o' tracks at sun up."

The Pirates (hesitating). "No—o—

Patsey. "I am; know where I kin get a six-shooter?"

The Pirates (almost ready to abandon piracy for bear hunting, but preserving their dignity). "Can't! We've runn'd away for real pirates."

Patsey. "Not for good."

The Queen (interposing with sad dignity and real tears in her round blue eyes). "Yes!" (slowly and shaking her head). "Can't go back again. Never! Never! Never! The—the—eye is cast!"

Patsey (bursting with excitement). "No'o! Sho'o! Wanter know."

The Pirates (a little frightened themselves, but tremulous with gratified vanity). "The Perleese is on our track!"

Patsey. "Lemme go with yer!"

Hickory. "Wot'll yer giv?"

Patsey. "Pistol and er bananer."

Hickory (with judicious prudence). "Let's see 'em."

Patsey was off like a shot; his bare little red feet trembling under him. In a few minutes he returned with an old fashioned revolver known as one of "Allen's pepper boxes" and a large banana. He was at once enrolled and the banana eaten.

As yet they had resolved on no definite nefarious plan. Hickory, looking down at Patsey's bare feet, instantly took off his own shoes. The bold act sent a thrill through his companions. Wan Lee took off his cloth leggings, Polly removed her shoes and stockings, but with royal foresight, tied them up in her handkerchief. The last link between them and civilization was broken.

"Let's go to the Slumgullion."

"Slumgullion" was the name given by the miners to certain soft, half-liquid mud, formed of the water and finely powdered earth that was carried off by the sluice boxes during gold washing, and eventually collected in a broad pool or lagoon before the outlet. There was a pool of this kind a quarter of a mile away, where there were "diggings" worked by Patsey's father, and thither they proceeded along the ridge in single file. When it was reached they solemnly began to wade in its viscid paint-like shallows. Possibly its unctuousness was pleasant to the touch; possibly there was a fascination in the fact that their parents had forbidden them to go near it, but probably the principal object of this performance was to produce a thick coating of mud on the feet and ankles, which, when dried in the sun, was supposed to harden the skin and render their shoes superfluous. It was also felt to be the first real step towards independence; they looked down at their ensanguined extremities and recognized the impossibility of their ever again crossing (unwashed) the family threshold.

Then they again hesitated. There was a manifest need of some well defined piratical purpose. The last act was reckless and irretrievable, but it was vague. They gazed at each other. There was a stolid look of resigned and superior tolerance in Wan Lee's eyes. Polly's glance wandered down the side of the slope to the distant little tunnels or openings made by the miners who were at work in the bowels of the mountain. "I'd like to go into one of them funny holes," she said to herself, half aloud.

Wan Lee suddenly began to blink his eyes with unwonted excitement. "Catchee tunnel—heap gold," he said, quickly. "When manee come outside to catchee dinner—Pilats go inside catchee tunnel! Shabee! Pilats catchee gold allee samee Melican man!"

"And take perseshiun," said Hickory.

"And hoist the Pirate flag," said Patsey.

"And build a fire, and cook, and have a family," said Polly.

The idea was fascinating to the point of being irresistible. The eyes of the four children became rounder and rounder. They seized each other's hands and swung them backwards and forwards, occasionally lifting their legs in a solemn rhythmic movement known only to childhood.

"Its orful far off!" said Patsey with a sudden look of dark importance. "Pap sez its free miles on the road. Take all day ter get there."

The bright faces were overcast.

"Less go down er slide!" said Hickory, boldly.

They approached the edge of the cliff. The "slide" was simply a sharp incline zigzagging down the side of the mountain used for sliding goods and provisions from the summit to the tunnel men at the different openings below. The continual traffic had gradually worn a shallow gulley half filled with earth and gravel into the face of the mountain which checked the momentum of the goods in their downward passage, but afforded no foothold for a pedestrian. No one had ever been known to descend a slide. That feat was evidently reserved for the Pirate band. They approached the edge of the slide hand in hand, hesitated—and the next moment disappeared!

Five minutes later the tunnel men of the Excelsior mine, a mile below, taking their luncheon on the rude platform of *débris* before their tunnel, were suddenly driven to shelter in the tunnel from an apparent rain of stones, and rocks, and pebbles, from the cliffs above. Looking up, they were startled at seeing four round objects revolving and bounding in the dust of the slide, which eventually resolved themselves into three boys and a girl. For a moment the good men held their breath in helpless terror. Twice, one of the children, had struck the outer edge of the bank and displaced stones that shot a thousand feet down into the dizzy depths of the valley! and now, one of them, the girl, had actually rolled out of the slide and was hanging over the chasm supported only by a clump of chimasal to which she clung!

"Hang on by your eyelids, Sis! but don't stir for Heaven's sake!" shouted one of the men, as two others started on a hopeless ascent of the cliff above them.

But a light childish laugh from the clinging little figure seemed to mock them! Then two small heads appeared at the edge of the slide; then a diminutive figure whose feet were apparently held by some invisible companion, was shoved over the brink and stretched its tiny arms towards the girl. But in vain, the distance was too great. Another laugh of intense youthful enjoyment followed the failure, and a new insecurity was added to the situation by the unsteady hands and

shoulders of the relieving party who were apparently shaking with laughter. Then the extended figure was seen to detach what looked like a small black rope from its shoulders and throw it to the girl. There was another little giggle. The faces of the men below paled in terror. Then Polly—for it was she—hanging to the long pig-tail of Wan Lee, was drawn with fits of laughter back in safety to the slide. Their childish treble of appreciation was answered by a ringing cheer from below.

"Darned ef I want to cut off a Chinaman's pig-tail again, boys," said one of the tunnel men as he went back to dinner.

Meantime the children had reached the goal and stood before the opening of one of the tunnels. Then these four heroes who had looked with cheerful levity on the deadly peril of their descent became suddenly frightened at the mysterious darkness of the cavern and turned pale at its threshold.

"Mebbee a wicked Joss backside holee, He catchee Pilats," said Wan Lee, gravely.

Hickory began to whimper, Patsey drew back, Polly alone stood her ground, albeit with a trembling lip.

"Let's say our prayers and frighten it away," she said, stoutly.

"No! No!" said Wan Lee, with sudden alarm. "No frighten Spillits! You waitee! Chinee boy he talkee Spillit not to frighten you."*

Tucking his hands under his blue blouse, Wan Lee suddenly produced from some mysterious recess of his clothing a quantity of red paper slips which he scattered at the entrance of the cavern. Then drawing from the same inexhaustible receptable certain squibs or fireworks, he let them off and threw them into the opening. There they went off with a slight fiz and splutter, a momentary glittering of small points in the darkness and a strong smell of gunpowder. Polly gazed at the

* The Chinese pray devoutly to the Evil Spirits *not* to injure them.

spectacle with undisguised awe and fascination. Hickory and Patsey breathed hard with satisfaction; it was beyond their wildest dreams of mystery and romance. Even Wan Lee appeared transfigured into a superior being by the potency of his own spells. But an unaccountable disturbance of some kind in the dim interior of the tunnel quickly drew the blood from their blanched cheeks again. It was a sound like coughing followed by something like an oath.

"He's made the Evil Spirit orful sick," said Hickory, in a loud whisper.

A slight laugh that to the children seemed demoniacal, followed.

"See," said Wan Lee, "Evil Spillet be likee Chinee, try talkee him."

The Pirates looked at Wan Lee not without a certain envy of this manifest favouritism. A fearful desire to continue their awful experiments, instead of pursuing their piratical avocations, was taking possession of them; but Polly, with one of the swift transitions of childhood, immediately began to extemporise a house for the party at the mouth of the tunnel, and, with parental foresight, gathered the fragments of the squibs to build a fire for supper. That frugal meal consisting of half a ginger biscuit, divided into five small portions, each served on a chip of wood, and having a deliciously mysterious flavour of gunpowder and smoke, was soon over. It was necessary after this, that the Pirates should at once seek repose after a day of adventure, which they did for the space of forty seconds in singularly impossible attitudes and far too aggressive snoring. Indeed, Master Hickory's almost upright *pose*, with tightly folded arms, and darkly frowning brows was felt to be dramatic, but impossible for a longer period. The brief interval enabled Polly to collect herself and to look around her in her usual motherly fashion. Suddenly she started and uttered a cry. In the excitement of the descent she had quite overlooked her doll, and was now regarding it with round-eyed horror!

"Lady Mary's hair's gone!" she cried, convulsively grasping the Pirate Hickory's legs.

Hickory at once recognized the battered doll under the aristocratic title which Polly had long ago bestowed upon it. He stared at the bald and battered head.

"Ha! ha!" he said, hoarsely; "skelped by Injins!"

For an instant the delicious suggestion soothed the imaginative Polly. But it was quickly dispelled by Wan Lee

"Lady Maley's pig-tail hangee top side hillee. Catchee on big quartz stone allee same Polly, me go fetchee."

"No!" quickly shrieked the others. The prospect of being left in the proximity of Wan Lee's evil spirit, without Wan Lee's exorcising power, was anything but reassuring. "No, don't go!" Even Polly (dropping a maternal tear on the bald head of Lady Mary) protested against this breaking up of the little circle. "Go to bed," she said, authoritatively, "and sleep until morning."

Thus admonished, the pirates again retired. This time effectively, for worn by actual fatigue or soothed by the delicious coolness of the cave, they gradually, one by one, succumbed to real slumber. Polly withheld from joining them, by official and maternal responsibility sat and blinked at them affectionately.

Gradually she, too, felt herself yielding to the fascination and mystery of the place and the solitude that encompassed her. Beyond the pleasant shadows where she sat, she saw the great world of mountain and valley through a dreamy haze that seemed to rise from the depths below and occasionally hang before the cavern like a veil. Long waves of spicy heat rolling up the mountain from the valley brought her the smell of pine trees and bay, and made the landscape swim before her eyes. She could hear the far off cry of teamsters on some unseen road; she could see the far off cloud of dust following the mountain stage coach, whose rattling wheels she could not hear. She felt very lonely, but was not quite afraid; she felt very melancholy, but was not entirely sad. And she could have easily awakened her sleeping companions if she wished.

No! She was a lone widow with nine children, six of whom were already in the lone churchyard on the hill, and the others lying ill with measles and scarlet fever beside her. She had just walked many weary miles that day, and had often begged from door to door for a slice of bread for the starving little ones. It was of no use now—they would die! They would never see their dear mother again. This was a favourite imaginative situation of Polly's, but only indulged when her companions were asleep, partly because she could not trust confederates with her more serious fancies, and partly because they were at such times passive in her hands. She glanced timidly round; satisfied that no one could observe her, she softly visited the bedside of each of her companions, and administered from a purely fictitious bottle spoonfuls of invisible medicine. Physical correction in the form of slight taps, which they always required, and in which Polly was strong, was only withheld now from a sense of their weak condition. But in vain, they succumbed to the fell disease—(they always died at this juncture)—and Polly was left alone. She thought of the little church where she had once seen a funeral, and remembered the nice smell of the flowers; she dwelt with melancholy satisfaction on the nine little tombstones in the graveyard, each with an inscription, and looked forward with gentle anticipation to the long summer days when, with Lady Mary in her lap, she would sit on those graves clad in the deepest mourning. The fact that the unhappy victims at times moved as it were uneasily in their graves or snored, did not affect Polly's imaginative contemplation, nor withhold the tears that gathered in her round eyes.

Presently the lids of the round eyes began to droop, the landscape beyond began to grow more confused, and sometimes to disappear entirely and reappear again with startling distinctness. Then a sound of rippling water from the little stream that flowed from the mouth of the tunnel soothed her and seemed to carry her away with it, and then everything was dark.

The next thing she remembered was that she was apparently being carried along on some gliding object to the sound of rippling water. She was not alone, for her three companions were lying beside her, rather tightly packed and squeezed in the same mysterious vehicle. Even in the profound darkness that surrounded her, Polly could feel and hear that they were accompanied, and once or twice a faint streak of light from the side of the tunnel showed her gigantic shadows walking slowly on either side of the gliding car. She felt the little hands of her associates seeking hers, and knew they were awake and conscious, and she returned to each a reassuring pressure from the large protecting instinct of her maternal little heart. Presently the car glided into an open space of bright light, and stopped. The transition from the darkness of the tunnel at first dazzled their eyes. It was like a dream.

They were in a circular cavern from which three other tunnels like the one they had passed through, diverged. The walls, lit up by fifty or sixty candles stuck at irregular intervals in crevices of the rock, were of glittering quartz and mica. But more remarkable than all were the inmates of the cavern, who were ranged round the walls; men, who like their attendants, seemed to be of extra stature; who had blackened faces, wore red bandanna handkerchiefs round their heads and their waists, and carried enormous knives and pistols stuck in their belts. On a raised platform made of a packing box, on which was rudely painted a skull and cross bones, sat the chief or leader of the band covered with a buffalo robe; on either side of him were two small barrels marked "Grog" and "Gunpowder." The children stared and clung closer to Polly. Yet, in spite of these desperate and warlike accessories, the strangers bore a singular resemblance to "Christy Minstrels" in their blackened faces and attitudes that somehow made them seem less awful. In particular, Polly was impressed with the fact that even the most ferocious had a certain kindliness of eye, and showed their teeth almost idiotically.

"Welcome," said the leader. "Welcome to the Pirate's Cave! The Red Rover of the North Fork of the Stanislaus River salutes the Queen of the Pirate Isle!" He rose up and made an extraordinary bow. It was repeated by the others with more or less exaggeration to the point of one humourist losing his balance!

"O, thank you very much," said Polly, timidly, but drawing her little flock closer to her with a small protecting arm; "but could you—would you—please—tell us—what time it is?"

"We are approaching the Middle of Next Week," said the leader, gravely; "but what of that? Time is made for slaves! The Red Rover seeks it not! Why should the Queen?"

"I think we must be going," hesitated Polly, yet by no means displeased with the recognition of her rank.

"Not until we have paid homage to your Majesty," returned the leader. "What ho! there! Let Brother Step-and-Fetch-It pass the Queen around that we may do her honour." Observing that Polly shrank slightly back, he added: "Fear nothing, the man who hurts a hair of Her Majesty's head, dies by this hand. Ah! ha!"

The others all said, ha! ha! and danced alternately on one leg and then on the other, but always with the same dark resemblance to Christy Minstrels. Brother Step-and-Fetch-It, whose very long beard had a confusing suggestion of being a part of the leader's buffalo robe, lifted her gently in his arms and carried her to the Red Rovers in turn. Each one bestowed a kiss upon her cheek or forehead, and would have taken her in his arms, or on his knees, or otherwise lingered over his salute, but they were sternly restrained by their leader. When the solemn rite was concluded, Step-and-Fetch-It paid his own courtesy with an extra squeeze of the curly head, and deposited her again in the truck—a little frightened, a little astonished, but with a considerable accession to her dignity. Hickory and Patsey looked on with stupefied amazement. Wan Lee alone remained stolid and unimpressed, regarding the scene with calm and triangular eyes.

"Will Your Majesty see the Red Rover's dance?"

"No, if you please," said Polly, with gentle seriousness.

"Will Your Majesty fire this barrel of Gunpowder, or tap this breaker of Grog?"

"No, I thank you."

"Is there no command Your Majesty would lay upon us?"

"No, please," said Polly, in a failing voice.

"Is there anything Your Majesty has lost? Think again! Will Your Majesty deign to cast your royal eyes on this?"

He drew from under his buffalo robe what seemed like a long tress of blond hair, and held it aloft. Polly instantly recognized the missing scalp of her hapless doll.

"If you please, Sir, it's Lady Mary's. She's lost it."

"And lost it—Your Majesty—only to find something more precious! Would Your Majesty hear the story?"

A little alarmed, a little curious, a little self-anxious, and a little induced by the nudges and pinches of her companions, the Queen blushingly signified her royal assent.

"Enough. Bring refreshments. Will Your Majesty prefer winter-green, peppermint, rose, or accidulated drops? Red or white? Or perhaps Your Majesty will let me recommend these bull's eyes," said the leader, as a collection of sweets in a hat were suddenly produced from the barrel labelled "Gunpowder" and handed to the children.

"Listen," he continued, in a silence broken only by the gentle sucking of bull's eyes. "Many years ago the old Red Rovers of these parts locked up all their treasures in a secret cavern in this mountain. They used spells and magic to keep it from being entered or found by anybody, for there was a certain mark upon it made by a peculiar rock that stuck out of it, which signified what there was below. Long afterwards, other Red Rovers who had heard of it, came here and spent days and days trying to discover it; digging holes and blasting tunnels like this, but of no use! Sometimes they thought they discovered the magic marks in the peculiar rock that stuck out of it, but when they dug there they found no treasure. And why? Because there was a magic spell upon it. And what was that magic spell? Why, this! It could only be discovered by a person who could not possibly know that he or she had discovered it, who never could or would be able to enjoy it, who could never see it, never feel it, never, in fact know anything at all about it! It wasn't a dead man, it wasn't an animal, it wasn't a baby!"

"Why," said Polly, jumping up and clapping her hands, "it was a Dolly."

"Your Majesty's head is level! Your Majesty has guessed it!" said the leader, gravely. "It was Your Majesty's own dolly, Lady Mary, who broke the spell! When Your Majesty came down the slide, the doll fell from your gracious hand when your foot slipped. Your Majesty recovered Lady Mary, but did not observe that her hair had caught in a peculiar rock, called the 'Outcrop,' and remained behind! When, later on, while sitting with your attendants at the mouth of the tunnel, Your Majesty discovered that Lady Mary's hair was gone; I overheard Your Majesty, and despatched the trusty Step-and-Fetch-It to seek it at the mountain side. He did so, and found it clinging to the rock, and beneath it—the entrance to the Secret Cave!"

Patsey and Hickory, who, failing to understand a word of this explanation, had given themselves up to the unconstrained enjoyment of the sweets, began now to apprehend that some change was impending, and prepared for the worst by hastily swallowing what they had in their mouths, thus defying enchantment, and getting ready for speech. Polly, who had closely followed the story, albeit with the embellishments of her own imagination, made her eyes rounder than ever. A bland smile broke on Wan Lee's face, as, to the children's amazement, he quietly disengaged himself from the group and stepped before the leader.

"Melican man plenty foolee Melican chillern. No foolee China boy! China boy knowee you. *You* no Led Lofer. *You* no Pilat—you allee same tunnel man—you Bob Johnson! Me shabbee you! You dressee up allee same as Led Lofer—but you Bob Johnson—allee same. My fader washee washee for you. You no payee him. You owee him folty dolla! Me blingee you billee. You no payee billee! You say, 'Chalkee up, John.' You say, 'Bimeby, John.' But me no catchee folty dolla!"

A roar of laughter followed, in which even the leader apparently forgot himself enough to join. But the next moment springing to his feet, he shouted, "Ho! ho! A traitor! Away with him to the deepest dungeon beneath the castle moat!"

Hickory and Patsey began to whimper. But Polly, albeit with a tremulous lip, stepped to the side of her little Pagan friend. "Don't you dare to touch him," she said, with a shake of unexpected determination in her little curly head; "if you do, I'll tell my father, and he will slay you! All of you—there!"

"Your father! Then you are *not* the Queen!"

It was a sore struggle to Polly to abdicate her royal position, it was harder to do it with befitting dignity. To evade the direct question she was obliged to abandon her defiant attitude. "If you please, Sir," she said, hurriedly, with an increasing colour and no stops, "we're not always pirates, you know, and Wan Lee is only our boy what brushes my shoes in the morning, and runs of errands, and he doesn't mean anything bad, Sir, and we'd like to take him back home with us."

"Enough," said the leader, changing his entire manner with the most sudden and shameless inconsistency. "You shall go back together, and woe betide the miscreant who would prevent it. What say you brothers? What shall be his fate who dares to separate our noble Queen from her faithful Chinese henchman?"

"He shall die!" roared the others, with beaming cheerfulness.

"And what say you—shall we see them home?"

"We will!" roared the others.

Before the children could fairly comprehend what had passed, they were again lifted into the truck and began to glide back into the tunnel they had just quitted. But not again in darkness and silence; the entire band of Red Rovers accompanied them, illuminating the dark passage with the candles they had snatched from the walls. In a few moments they were at the entrance again. The great world lay beyond them once more with rocks and valleys suffused by the rosy light of the setting sun. The past seemed like a dream.

But were they really awake now? They could not tell. They accepted everything with the confidence and credulity of all children who have no experience to compare with their first impressions and to whom the future contains nothing impossible. It was without surprise, therefore, that they felt themselves lifted on the shoulders of the men who were making quite a procession along the steep trail towards the settlement again. Polly noticed that at the mouth of the other tunnels they were greeted by men as if they were carrying tidings of great joy; that they stopped to rejoice together, and that in some mysterious manner their conductors had got their faces

washed, and had become more like beings of the outer world. When they neared the settlement the excitement seemed to have become greater; people rushed out to shake hands with the men who were carrying them, and overpowered even the children with questions they could not understand. Only one sentence Polly could clearly remember as being the burden of all congratulations. "Struck the old lead at last!" With a faint consciousness that she knew something about it, she tried to assume a dignified attitude on the leader's shoulders even while she was beginning to be heavy with sleep.

And then she remembered a crowd near her father's house, out of which her father came smiling pleasantly on her, but not interfering with her triumphal progress until the leader finally deposited her in her mother's lap in their own sitting room. And then she remembered being "cross" and declining to answer any questions, and shortly afterwards found herself comfortably in bed. Then she heard her mother say to her father:—

"It really seems too ridiculous for any thing, John, the idea of these grown men dressing themselves up to play with children."

"Ridiculous or not," said her father, "these grown men of the 'Excelsior' mine have just struck the famous old lode of Red Mountain, which is as good as a fortune to everybody on the Ridge, and were as wild as boys! And they say it never would have been found if Polly hadn't tumbled over the slide directly on top of the outcrop, and left the absurd wig of that wretched doll of hers to mark its site."

"And that," murmured Polly sleepily to her doll as she drew it closer to her breast, "is all that they know of it."

THE PIED PIPER OF HAMELIN

Poem by Robert Browning

his tale was written four years before Kate Greenaway was born, and she loved reciting it as a child. In 1882, through Frederick Locker, she met Browning, then seventy, and made great friends with both the poet and his sister. In 1888 Kate made colour illustrations for this children's edition, which became one of her best-known and most rewarding works. It was, incidentally, the only period piece she undertook, and in deference to the medieval setting she dressed the men in tunics; otherwise the costumes are more or less pure Greenaway.

"It's all good and nice as it can be," said Ruskin. "The piper is sublime—and the children lovely."

Kate Greenaway had to find many models for her illustrations, the crowd scenes being on a larger scale than anything she had attempted before. In the past, her brother John, her father, mother, and Fanny had often sat for her; so had young friends. At other times she picked models from the schoolroom, or hired professionals to pose. With her great good humour, tact, patience, and her winning personality, she always succeeded in getting the most out of them.

Edmund Evans printed the book originally, and George Routledge published it. In 1900 Frederick Warne brought out a reissue, which has been reprinted scores of times since.

I.

HAMELIN Town's in Brunswick,
By famous Hanover city;
  The river Weser, deep and wide,
  Washes its wall on the southern side;
  A pleasanter spot you never spied;
But, when begins my ditty,
  Almost five hundred years ago,
  To see the townsfolk suffer so
    From vermin, was a pity.

II.

  Rats!
They fought the dogs and killed the cats,
  And bit the babies in the cradles,
And ate the cheeses out of the vats,
  And licked the soup from the cook's
    own ladles,
Split open the kegs of salted sprats,
Made nests inside men's Sunday hats,
And even spoiled the women's chats,
  By drowning their speaking
  With shrieking and squeaking
In fifty different sharps and flats.

106

III.

At last the people in a body
    To the Town Hall came flocking:
" 'Tis clear," cried they, "our Mayor's a noddy;
    "And as for our Corporation—shocking
"To think we buy gowns lined with ermine
"For dolts that can't or won't determine
"What's best to rid us of our vermin!
"You hope, because you're old and obese,
"To find in the furry civic robe ease?
"Rouse up, sirs! Give your brains a racking
"To find the remedy we're lacking,
"Or, sure as fate, we'll send you packing!"
At this the Mayor and Corporation
Quaked with a mighty consternation.

IV.

An hour they sate in council,
    At length the Mayor broke silence:
"For a guilder I'd my ermine gown sell;
    "I wish I were a mile hence!
"It's easy to bid one rack one's brain—
"I'm sure my poor head aches again,
"I've scratched it so, and all in vain.
"Oh for a trap, a trap, a trap!"
Just as he said this, what should hap
At the chamber door but a gentle tap?
"Bless us," cried the Mayor, "what's that?"
(With the Corporation as he sat,
Looking little though wondrous fat;
Nor brighter was his eye, nor moister
Than a too-long-opened oyster,
Save when at noon his paunch grew mutinous
For a plate of turtle green and glutinous)
"Only a scraping of shoes on the mat?
"Anything like the sound of a rat
"Makes my heart go pit-a-pat!"

V.

"Come in!"—the Mayor cried, looking bigger:
And in did come the strangest figure!
His queer long coat from heel to head
Was half of yellow and half of red,
And he himself was tall and thin,
With sharp blue eyes, each like a pin,
And light loose hair, yet swarthy skin,
No tuft on cheek nor beard on chin,
But lips where smiles went out and in;
There was no guessing his kith and kin:

And nobody could enough admire
The tall man and his quaint attire.
Quoth one: "It's as my great-grandsire,
"Starting up at the Trump of Doom's tone,
"Had walked this way from his painted tombstone!"

VI.

He advanced to the council-table:
And, "Please your honours," said he, "I'm able,
"By means of a secret charm, to draw
"All creatures living beneath the sun,
"That creep or swim or fly or run,
"After me so as you never saw!
"And I chiefly use my charm
"On creatures that do people harm,
"The mole and toad and newt and viper;
"And people call me the Pied Piper."
(And here they noticed round his neck
A scarf of red and yellow stripe,
To match with his coat and the self-same cheque;
And at the scarf's end hung a pipe;
And his fingers they noticed were ever straying
As if impatient to be playing
Upon this pipe, as low it dangled
Over his vesture so old-fangled.)
"Yet," said he, "poor Piper as I am,
"In Tartary I freed the Cham,
"Last June, from his huge swarms of gnats;
"I eased in Asia the Nizam
"Of a monstrous brood of vampyre-bats:

110

"And as for what your brain bewilders,
"If I can rid your town of rats
"Will you give me a thousand guilders?"
"One? fifty thousand!"—was the exclamation
Of the astonished Mayor and Corporation.

VII.

Into the street the Piper stept,
  Smiling first a little smile,
As if he knew what magic slept
  In his quiet pipe the while;
Then, like a musical adept,
To blow the pipe his lips he wrinkled,
And green and blue his sharp eyes twinkled,
Like a candle-flame where salt is sprinkled;
And ere three shrill notes the pipe uttered,
You heard as if an army muttered;
And the muttering grew to a grumbling;
And the grumbling grew to a mighty rumbling;
And out of the houses the rats came tumbling.
Great rats, small rats, lean rats, brawny rats,
Brown rats, black rats, grey rats, tawny rats,
Grave old plodders, gay young friskers,
  Fathers, mothers, uncles, cousins,
Cocking tails and pricking whiskers,
  Families by tens and dozens,
Brothers, sisters, husbands, wives—
Followed the Piper for their lives.
From street to street he piped advancing,
And step for step they followed dancing,
Until they came to the river Weser
Wherein all plunged and perished!
—Save one who, stout as Julius Cæsar,
Swam across and lived to carry
(As he, the manuscript he cherished)
To Rat-land home his commentary:
Which was, "At the first shrill notes of the
        pipe,
"I heard a sound as of scraping tripe,
"And putting apples, wondrous ripe,
"Into a cider-press's gripe:
"And a moving away of pickle-tub-boards,
"And a leaving ajar of conserve-cupboards,
"And a drawing the corks of train-oil-flasks,
"And a breaking the hoops of butter-casks:
"And it seemed as if a voice
"(Sweeter far than by harp or by psaltery
"Is breathed) called out, 'Oh rats, rejoice!
" 'The world is grown to one vast drysaltery!

" 'So munch on, crunch on, take your nuncheon,
" 'Breakfast, supper, dinner, luncheon!'
"And just as a bulky sugar-puncheon,
"Already staved, like a great sun shone
"Glorious scarce an inch before me,
"Just as methought it said, 'Come, bore me!'
"—I found the Weser rolling o'er me."

VIII.

You should have heard the Hamelin people
Ringing the bells till they rocked the steeple.
"Go," cried the Mayor, "and get long poles,
"Poke out the nest and block up the holes!
"Consult with carpenters and builders,
"And leave in our town not even a trace
"Of the rats!"—when suddenly, up the face
Of the Piper perked in the market-place,
With a, "First, if you please, my thousand
      guilders!"

IX.

A thousand guilders! The Mayor looked blue;
So did the Corporation too.
For council dinners made rare havoc
With Claret, Moselle, Vin-de-Grave, Hock;
And half the money would replenish
Their cellar's biggest butt with Rhenish.
To pay this sum to a wandering fellow
With a gipsy coat of red and yellow!
"Beside," quoth the Mayor with a knowing wink,
"Our business was done at the river's brink;
"We saw with our eyes the vermin sink,
"And what's dead can't come to life, I think.
"So, friend, we're not the folks to shrink
"From the duty of giving you something to drink,
"And a matter of money to put in your poke;
"But as for the guilders, what we spoke
"Of them, as you very well know, was a joke.
"Beside, our losses have made us thrifty.
"A thousand guilders! Come, take fifty!"

X.

The Piper's face fell, and he cried,
"No trifling! I can't wait, beside!
"I've promised to visit by dinner-time
"Bagdad, and accept the prime
"Of the Head-Cook's pottage, all he's rich in,
"For having left, in the Caliph's kitchen,

112

"Of a nest of scorpions no survivor:
"With him I proved no bargain-driver,
"With you, don't think I'll bate a stiver!
"And folks who put me in a passion
"May find me pipe after another fashion."

XI.

"How?" cried the Mayor, "d'ye think I brook
"Being worse treated than a Cook?
"Insulted by a lazy ribald
"With idle pipe and vesture piebald?
"You threaten us, fellow? Do your worst,
"Blow your pipe there till you burst!"

XII.

Once more he stept into the street,
    And to his lips again
Laid his long pipe of smooth straight cane;
    And ere he blew three notes (such sweet
Soft notes as yet musician's cunning
    Never gave the enraptured air)
There was a rustling, that seemed like a bustling
Of merry crowds justling at pitching and hustling,
Small feet were pattering, wooden shoes clattering,
Little hands clapping and little tongues chattering.
And, like fowls in a farm-yard when barley is
        scattering,
Out came the children running.
All the little boys and girls,
With rosy cheeks and flaxen curls,
And sparkling eyes and teeth like pearls,
Tripping and skipping, ran merrily after
The wonderful music with shouting and laughter.

XIII.

The Mayor was dumb, and the Council stood
As if they were changed into blocks of wood,
Unable to move a step, or cry
To the children merrily skipping by,
—Could only follow with the eye
That joyous crowd at the Piper's back.
But how the Mayor was on the rack,
And the wretched Council's bosoms beat,

114

As the Piper turned from the High Street
To where the Weser rolled its waters
Right in the way of their sons and daughters!
However he turned from South to West,
And to Koppelberg Hill his steps addressed,
And after him the children pressed;
Great was the joy in every breast.

117

"He never can cross that mighty top!
"He's forced to let the piping drop,
"And we shall see our children stop!"
When, lo, as they reached the mountain-side,
A wondrous portal opened wide,
As if a cavern was suddenly hollowed;
And the Piper advanced and the children followed,
And when all were in to the very last,
The door in the mountain-side shut fast.
Did I say, all? No! One was lame,
And could not dance the whole of the way;
And in after years, if you would blame
His sadness, he was used to say,—
"It's dull in our town since my playmates left!
"I can't forget that I'm bereft
"Of all the pleasant sights they see,
"Which the Piper also promised me.
"For he led us, he said, to a joyous land,
"Joining the town and just at hand,
"Where waters gushed and fruit-trees grew,
"And flowers put forth a fairer hue,
"And everything was strange and new;
"The sparrows were brighter than peacocks here,
"And their dogs outran our fallow deer,
"And honey-bees had lost their stings,
"And horses were born with eagles' wings:
"And just as I became assured
"My lame foot would be speedily cured,
"The music stopped and I stood still,
"And found myself outside the hill,
"Left alone against my will,
"To go now limping as before,
"And never hear of that country more!"

XIV.

Alas, alas for Hamelin!
   There came into many a burgher's pate
   A text which says that Heaven's gate
   Opes to the rich at as easy rate
As the needle's eye takes a camel in!
The Mayor sent East, West, North, and South,
To offer the Piper, by word of mouth,
   Wherever it was men's lot to find him,
Silver and gold to his heart's content,
If he'd only return the way he went,
   And bring the children behind him.
But when they saw 'twas a lost endeavour,
And Piper and dancers were gone for ever,
They made a decree that lawyers never
   Should think their records dated duly

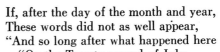

If, after the day of the month and year,
These words did not as well appear,
"And so long after what happened here
    "On the Twenty-second of July,
"Thirteen hundred and seventy-six":
And the better in memory to fix
The place of the children's last retreat,
They called it, the Pied Piper's Street—
Where any one playing on pipe or tabor,
Was sure for the future to lose his labour.
Nor suffered they hostelry or tavern

To shock with mirth a street so solemn;
But opposite the place of the cavern
    They wrote the story on a column,
And on the great church-window painted
The same, to make the world acquainted
How their children were stolen away,
And there it stands to this very day.
And I must not omit to say
That in Transylvania there's a tribe
Of alien people that ascribe
The outlandish ways and dress
On which they neighbours lay such stress,
To their fathers and mothers having risen
Out of some subterraneous prison
Into which they were trepanned
Long time ago in a mighty band
Out of Hamelin town in Brunswick land,
But how or why, they don't understand.

xv.

So, Willy, let me and you be wipers
Of scores out with all men—especially pipers!
And, whether they pipe us free from rats or
    ·from mice,
If we've promised them aught, let us keep
    our promise!

KATE GREENAWAY'S BOOK OF GAMES

"What a joy . . . entering Nanny's domain to find the children so happily occupied . . . and everything pretty as a Kate Greenaway picture," a proud Victorian parent once remarked. That was in the days of large families and huge households, when help was plentiful upstairs as well as down.

Miss Greenaway knew what children liked, also what parents, who bought their books, liked. For that reason, if for no other, her characters were always exemplary. No cheating, pushing, no tantrums or tears. Not here. This is the way young ladies and gentlemen were expected to play games.

The original sixty-four-page book, describing fifty-three games and illustrating twenty-four in colour, was published in 1889.

TOM TIDDLER'S GROUND

ONE part of the field or lawn is marked off as Tom Tiddler's ground, over which Tom presides in solitary state. It is supposed to have a quantity of lumps of gold scattered about it. The other players venture on, and pretend to be picking up something, at the same time singing: "Here I am on Tom Tiddler's ground, picking up gold and silver!" He rushes after them, and if he succeeds in catching anybody, that one has to take his place as Tom Tiddler. Tom may not leave his own ground.

HUNT THE SLIPPER

THE children sit on the ground, or on low seats in a circle, with their knees raised. One has been left out; she brings a slipper, and giving it to one child says:—

> "Cobbler, cobbler, mend, my shoe,
> Get it done by half-past two."

She goes away, and comes back in about a minute and asks if it is done. (During this time the slipper has been passing round.) The child answers, she thinks her neighbour has it; so the seeker passes on to her, and getting the same answer she has to go round till the slipper is found. If she is a long time finding it, the slipper may be thrown across the circle.

MUSICAL CHAIRS

SOMEONE plays the piano. Chairs must be placed down the room, back to back, one less in number than the players who galop round them in time to the music. Suddenly it stops, and everybody then tries to get a chair, but as there is one short someone will be left standing, and is then out of the game. A chair is taken away and the game goes on as before till only one player, the victor, is left.

KING OF THE CASTLE

ONE player ascends a little hillock and calls himself "King of the Castle"; the others immediately try to pull or push him off, while he strives to the utmost to repel them and retain his position. The player who succeeds in deposing him, becomes "King of the Castle" in his place.

PUSS IN THE CORNER

THE child who represents puss stands in the middle, while the others stand at fixed stations round her. One then beckons to another saying: "Puss, puss, give me a drop of water!" when each runs and change places. Puss then runs and tries to get into one of the places; if she succeeds, the one left out is puss.

BLIND

MAN'S BUFF

BLIND MAN'S BUFF

ONE child has her eyes blindfolded with a handkerchief, so that she cannot see, and is placed in the middle of the room. The children say to her: "How many horses has your father got?" She replies: "Three!" Children: "What colours are they?" She: "Black, White, and Grey!" Children: "Turn round three times and catch who you may!" Then they turn her round three times, and she tries to catch anyone she can; the one caught has to be next "blind man."

QUEEN ANNE AND HER MAIDS

ONE child covers her eyes, while the others, standing in a row close to each other, put their hands behind them. One has a ball concealed, which all pretend to have. They then call the one who has covered her eyes, and addressing her sing:—

> "Queen Anne, Queen Anne, she sits in the sun;
> As fair as a lily, as brown as a bun;
> She sends you three letters, and begs you'll read one!"

To which Queen Anne replies:—

> "I cannot read one unless I read all,
> So please Miss Mabel* deliver the ball."

If she has guessed correctly, the one who had the ball takes Queen Anne's place; but if it was a wrong one she hides her eyes again while the ball changes hands.

* Or whatever the name of the one she thinks has it is.

125

THE APRIL BABY'S BOOK OF TUNES

With Text by "the Author of *Elizabeth and Her German Garden*" (Countess von Arnim)

go on liking things more and more, seeing them more and more beautiful. Don't you think it is a great possession to be able to get so much joy out of things that are always there to give it, and do not change?"

Kate Greenaway wrote this to Ruskin in September 1899, just before starting to make these illustrations.

Except for the *Almanacks*, it was her first book project in ten years. Her health was failing; yet, as has often been said, the sixteen colour drawings were "as fresh as if she had illustrated nursery rhymes for the first time." The book was not an Edmund Evans venture; Macmillan, for whom, in 1879, she had illustrated *The Heir of Redclyffe*, published it in the autumn of 1900.

LITTLE MISS MUFFET

Lit - tle Miss Muff - et sat on a tuff - et eat - ing her curds and

126

whey, When down came a spi - der and sat down be - side her, and fright-en'd Miss Muff - et a - way.

PUSSY CAT, PUSSY CAT

Quickly.

Puss - y Cat, Puss - y Cat, where have you been? I've been to Lon - don to look at the Queen. . .

Puss - y Cat, Puss - y Cat, what did you there? I fright-en'd a lit - tle mouse un - der the chair.

HUSH-A-BYE, BABY

Hush-a-bye, baby, on the tree top, When the wind blows the cra-dle will rock, When the bough

breaks the cra-dle will fall, and down comes ba-by and cra-dle and all.

LITTLE POLLY FLINDERS

Quickly.

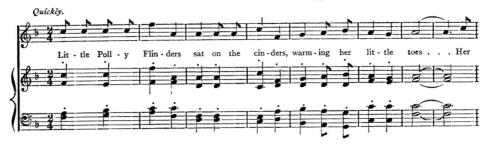

Lit-tle Poll-y Flin-ders sat on the cin-ders, warm-ing her lit-tle toes . . . Her

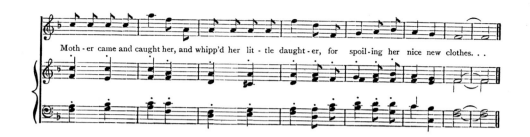

Moth-er came and caught her, and whipp'd her lit-tle daught-er, for spoil-ing her nice new clothes...

CURLY LOCKS

Curl-y locks, Curl-y locks, wilt thou be mine? Thou shalt not wash dish-es nor yet feed the swine, But sit on a

cush-ion and sew a fine seam, And feed up-on straw-berr-ies, su-gar, and cream.

JACK AND JILL

Jack and Jill went up the hill to fetch a pail of wa-ter, Jack fell

slowly . . . .

slowly . . . .

down and broke his crown, and Jill . . came tumb-ling af - - ter.

quicker . . . . . .

quicker . . . . . .

Ped.

WHERE ARE YOU GOING TO, MY PRETTY MAID?

Where are you going to, my pretty maid? I'm going a-milking, Sir, she said. May I go with you, my pretty maid? You're

kindly welcome, Sir, she said. Who is your father, my pretty maid? My father's a farmer, Sir, she said. Say will you

marry me, my pretty maid? Yes, if you please, kind Sir, she said. What is your fortune, my pretty maid? My

My face is my fortune, kind Sir, she said.
Then I won't marry you, my pretty maid!
Nobody ask'd you, Sir, she said.

"Taking in the Roses."
Watercolour originally
in the collection of
Stuart M. Samuel, M.P.

FAREWELLS

Things *are so* beautiful and wonderful, you feel there must be another life where you see more—hear more—and *know* more. All of it cannot die."

It was January 1896, and Kate Greenaway, now nearing fifty, had picked up her pen and for the many hundreth time had dutifully composed a letter to John Ruskin. He was in his seventy-seventh year, and well cared for by his adopted daughter, Mrs. Arthur Severn, or Joannie, as Kate had long since affectionately called this devoted friend.

Her visits to Brantwood would appear to have become rarer these days, and her letters to Ruskin and the Severn family all the more looked for when the postman made his morning rounds. Kate's spontaneous philosophic questionings; her comments about talents such as Aubrey Beardsley—whose work she *hated*—or about the older artists—whose paintings she worshipped; her chatter about her visits with Lady Jeune at Arlington Manor, or about the book she was currently reading; her ecstasies over the bunch of flowers Lady Mayo had popped through the front door; or, later, when she started to paint with oils, her struggles to make the paints behave; all of this, including running reports on her adored Rover, a retriever who basked in the overflow of her affections, greatly entertained Ruskin. He answered her letters in kind, but not always in the most kindly way. She was, he said, "a mixed child and woman and therefore extremely puzzling." He would flatter her by saying Donatello would have appreciated her, unhesitatingly to add, "You would do much more beautiful things if you refrained from being hurried away by the new thoughts which crowd upon you and hinder you from fully realising *any!*" Or, with exasperation, "You are always straining after a fancy instead of doing the thing as it is."

"The Fable of the Girl and Her Milk Pail." This watercolour by Kate Green-away, showing a pronounced Pre-Raphaelite influence, was originally exhibited at The Fine Arts Society, London, in January 1893, where it sold for forty-five guineas. At an auction in 1970 it fetched more than ten times that sum. (Private collection. Courtesy Sotheby Parke Bernet)

In a letter she had written Ruskin that past November, a sentence, so short it might have passed unnoticed, read: "I am never as strong as I was." Probably it was too early to recognize a trace of the "muscular rheumatism" that she was to compain of later—the ailment that became acute and so "horribly painful" towards the end of her life.

It had been a worrying year. Much against her better judgement, the 1895 *Almanack* had been made up of line drawings lifted from *The English Spelling-Book*. Charming though this little volume was, it didn't sell. This left Kate "in a state of great perplexity as to what work to do and what to agree about books." No almanack appeared in 1896, but the next year a new publisher, J. M. Dent, took a chance with *Kate Greenaway's Almanack for 1897*, and by Christmas wished he hadn't.

Apart from the Almanacks, no new Greenaway volume had come out since 1889, nor, it had begun to seem, would there ever be another. Then out of the blue came *The April Baby's Book of Tunes* in 1900. With this book a new wave of Greenaway popularity arose, but by then Kate was too unwell to take advantage of it.

Although the 1890s were lean years for her books, this was not so for her paintings; indeed, the public at last had the opportunity of seeing originals they had always longed to see, appropriately exhibited, furthermore, in august surroundings.

Her most fully developed period as a watercolourist might be said to have started in 1888. During this productive year she completed *The Pied Piper of Hamelin* illustrations and, among other projects, undertook a number of private commissions, notably those for Lady Maria Ponsonby, Lady Northcote, and Lady Nevill, who, again, eight years later, was to delight Kate by purchasing one of her drawings as a wedding present for Princess Maud of Wales and Prince Charles of Denmark—the couple who in 1905 were to become Norway's king and queen.

Another of Kate's patrons, often mentioned in the records, was a Member of Parliament, Stuart M. Samuel, for whom she later designed a book-plate, did a watercolour of his daughter, Vera, and painted a "procession"—a decorative garland of dancing children—for the family nursery.

In the past, also, Kate Greenaway had been sought by parents to do likenesses of their children. Even though she found portraits "so much more difficult . . . than a purely fancy drawing," she could not say *no*, for instance, to the attractive Frederick Lockers who, suddenly blessed with twins at Rowfant in 1881, sent her an enchanting little ditty, one verse of which ran:

> Yes, there they lie, so small, so quaint.
> Two mouths, two noses, and two chins—
> Which painter shall we get to paint
> And glorify the twins?

Kate remembered the twins in 1883, fondly dedicating *Little Ann* to them and to the other two Locker children as well.

In 1888, at a party at the Tennysons' in Belgrave Square, Kate had also again met an old student from Heartherley's, the former Helen Paterson, now Mrs. William Allingham, wife of the poet. Kate and Helen Allingham, in whose work certain similarities were to become apparent, took to the country on frequent painting expeditions and became the greatest of friends. More and more Kate became interested in easel painting and concerned about exhibition material, finding with Helen Allingham some of her favourite subjects—red brick cottages and landscapes in Surrey and Buckinghamshire.

Far from being "out of things," as she had once feared, Kate was into practically everything—for a while at least. In 1889, the year she was shown in Paris, The Royal Institute of Painters in Watercolours elected her a member, and her paintings were exhibited with this group in 1893 and again each year from 1894 to 1897. The big event of 1891, however, was her first one-man show of

"The Little Go-Cart." Watercolour drawing. (Originally in the Collection of J. Veitch)

her watercolour drawings at The Fine Arts Society, 148, New Bond Street. This big success was followed in 1894 by a slightly smaller exhibition at the gallery when her watercolour drawings grossed more than a thousand pounds—a proportionate and impressive achievement. Meanwhile, in 1892, Glasgow had seen twenty of her watercolours in the gallery of Messrs. Van Baerle.

It has been said that Kate Greenaway was once invited to America. If she ever toyed with the idea of travelling abroad, she kept it secret. The nearest she ever came to it was a visit to the Isle of Wight when the Allinghams were staying at Freshwater in 1890. The following year a friend named Mr. Anderson, connected with the Orient Line, for whom she decorated a guide, suggested that she take a holiday on their steamship *Garonne*, but nothing came of it. Never in her life was she to set foot out of England.

In this and other respects parallels can be drawn between Kate Greenaway and the queen-to-be of nursery books, Beatrix Potter, whose *Peter Rabbit* first bounded into the limelight in 1902. Both ladies were English and of Victorian background; both wrote and illustrated books that were—and still are—adored throughout the world; neither ventured abroad; both names became household words among children everywhere, and yet, neither Kate Greenaway (who never married) nor Beatrix Potter (who married late) had children of her own. One difference between the two was that Kate Greenaway drew children beautifully, while Beatrix Potter could hardly draw people at all, and, conversely, that Miss Potter drew animals beautifully, while Miss Greenaway had such trouble with them that she felt it the greatest triumph to manage even the likeness of a rat, quantities of which creatures she had to send scurrying across the pages of *The Pied Piper*—or *L'Homme à la Flute*, which her French publisher, Hachette & Cie, called this runaway best seller.

135

"Lucy Locket Lost her Pocket." (Private Collection)

Although America never saw Kate Greenaway, her books had been imported in ever-increasing thousands, and in 1893 a group of her original drawings and watercolours were to be admired, and bought (five of them), at Chicago's Columbian Exhibition. Shortly afterward *The Ladies' Home Journal* of Philadelphia, then with a 700,000 circulation, invited her to illustrate some verses by Laura E. Richards. These ran in the magazine between 1894 and 1896.

Once more she was represented in The Royal Academy, with a watercolour, "Baby Boy," in 1895, and once more in France—with a collection of drawings at the 1899 Paris Exhibition. A year earlier, however, a disappointed Kate Greenaway had written to Violet Dickinson: "I feel my kind of drawing is not the drawing that is liked, and also that I am getting to be a thing of the past." This short-lived fit of depression had been prompted by the fact that sixty-six of her watercolours, rather than the entire exhibition of one hundred and twenty-seven new pictures, had been sold at the 1898 Fine Arts Society show. At the same time the truth had to be admitted. In 1921 H. M. Cundall, in an appreciation of Kate Greenaway, pointed out that "a new, a more lasting influence had been brought about by the impressionism of Whistler and his followers." This, he said, "affected the sale of Kate Greenaway's little books, and their popularity for the moment waned."

In the 1890s inevitably there were sad farewells. Kate's father and mother had died, in 1890 and 1894 respectively, and in both instances it took her a long time to get over the loss. Her great friend Frederick Locker passed away in 1895. George du Maurier, artist and author of *Trilby*, whom she always considered "such a nice man," died in 1896. Two years later she saw her great friends the Tennysons for the last time as the family sailed for Australia, where the second Lord Tennyson had been appointed governor. In another two years came an even more severe though hardly unexpected blow. This was the death of the ailing John Ruskin. "I feel it very much," Kate remarked, "for he was a great friend . . . and there was no one else like him."

Most of Kate Greenaway's letters were decorated with spontaneous drawings such as this example she sent to Violet Dickinson.

Drawing for *The Ladies' Home Journal*.

"Study of a Boy." Drawing. (Courtesy London Borough of Camden)

Then, just after the nineteenth century had yielded to the twentieth, the figure who had dominated that golden age and whose name has remained synonymous with it, Queen Victoria, passed on. She was on the throne when Kate was born, and to have remained Queen until now made her the only crowned sovereign Kate was ever to know. By the time Victoria's eldest son, Edward VII, was crowned, Kate Greenaway herself had long since departed.

She died at her home, 39, Frognal, Hampstead, on November 6, 1901. After a cremation ceremony at Woking attended by members of the family and a few close friends, her ashes were interred at a cemetery in Hampstead.

"When I am dead," Kate Greenaway had written in a poem, "and all of you stand round and look upon me, my soul flown away . . . what beauteous land may I be wandering in . . . ?"

Among the countless eulogies that followed her death, that of her friend Austin Dobson would seem to have come closest to answering her:

> Farewell, kind heart. And if there be
> In that unshared Immensity
> Child-Angels, they will welcome thee.

138

From *Children of the Parsonage*
(1873).

From *Amateur Theatricals*
(1879).

From *Almanack for 1884.*

A LIST OF HER BOOKS

Those known to be wholly or partly illustrated by Kate Greenaway during her lifetime.

The following abbreviations have been used in the interest of conserving space: *Greenaway* for Illustrations by Kate Greenaway. Macmillan for Macmillan and Co. Ltd., London, and The Macmillan Company of New York. Routledge for George Routledge & Sons, London and New York. Warne for Frederick Warne & Co., Ltd., London and New York.

1867   INFANT AMUSEMENTS or *How to Make a Nursery Happy*. William H. G. Kingston. Frontis.: *Greenaway*. London: Griffith & Farran.

1870   AUNT LOUISA'S LONDON TOY BOOKS: DIAMONDS AND TOADS. *Greenaway*. Warne.
MY SCHOOL DAYS IN PARIS. Margaret S. Jeune. *Greenaway*. London: Griffith & Farran.

c. 1871 MADAME D'AULNOY'S FAIRY TALES: (1) THE FAIR ONE WITH GOLDEN LOCKS (2) THE BABES IN THE WOOD (3) TOM THUMB (4) BLUE BEARD (5) PUSS IN BOOTS (6) THE BLUE BIRD (7) THE WHITE CAT (8) HOP O' MY THUMB (9) RED RIDING HOOD. *Greenaway*. Edinburgh: Gall & Inglis.

1873   THE CHILDREN OF THE PARSONAGE. H. C. Selous. *Greenaway*. London: Griffith & Farran.

1874   FAIRY GIFTS or *A Wallet of Wonders*. *Greenaway*. London: Griffith & Farran. New York: E. P. Dutton.
A CALENDAR OF THE SEASONS FOR 1876. *Greenaway*. London: Marcus Ward.

1875   PUCK AND BLOSSOM. *A Fairy Tale*. Rosa Mulholland. *Greenaway*. London:
–1876   Marcus Ward.
THE FAIRY SPINNER. Miranda Hill. *Greenaway*. London: Marcus Ward.
A CRUISE IN THE ACORN. Alice Jerrold. *Greenaway*. London: Marcus Ward.
TURNASIDE COTTAGE. Mary Senior Clark. *Greenaway*. London: Marcus Ward.
MELCOMB MANOR: *A Family Chronicle*. Frederick Scarlett Potter. *Greenaway*. London: Marcus Ward.
CHILDREN'S SONGS. *Pictures and Music*. *Greenaway*. London: Marcus Ward.

1876   A CALENDAR OF THE SEASONS FOR 1877. *Greenaway*. London: Marcus Ward.
SEVEN BIRTHDAYS or *The Children of Fortune*. *A Fairy Chronicle*. Kathleen Knox. *Greenaway*. London: Griffith & Farran.

1877   THE QUIVER OF LOVE. *A Collection of Valentines*. Walter Crane and Kate Greenaway. Edited by W. J. Loftie. London: Marcus Ward.
TOM SEVEN YEARS OLD. H. Rutherford Russell. *Greenaway*. London: Marcus Ward.
STARLIGHT STORIES TOLD TO BRIGHT EYES AND LISTENING EARS. Fanny Lablache. *Greenaway*. London: Griffith & Farran.

1878   TOPO: *A Tale about English Children in Italy*. G. E. Brunefille (Lady Colin Campbell). *Greenaway*. London: Marcus Ward.
UNDER THE WINDOW. *Pictures and Rhymes for Children*. Kate Greenaway. Eng. and printed: Edmund Evans. Routledge. Re-issued 1900: Warne.

1879   THE HEIR OF REDCLYFFE. Charlotte M. Yonge. *Greenaway*. Macmillan.
AMATEUR THEATRICALS. Walter Herries Pollock and Lady Pollock. Edited by W. J. Loftie. Macmillan.
HEARTSEASE or *The Brother's Wife*. Charlotte M. Yonge. *Greenaway*. Macmillan.
TROT'S JOURNEY. *Pictures, Rhymes and Stories* (Taken from *Little Folks*). *Greenaway*. New York: R. Worthington.
TOYLAND, TROT'S JOURNEY *and Other Poems and Stories*. *Greenaway*. New York: R. Worthington.
THE LITTLE FOLKS' PAINTING BOOK. Verses and Stories: George Weatherly. Outline drawings for colouring: *Greenaway*. London, Paris, and New York: Cassell, Petter, Gilpin.

140

c. 1879 THE LITTLE FOLKS' NATURE PAINTING BOOK. Stories and verses: George Weatherly. Outline drawings for colouring: *Greenaway*. London, Paris, and New York: Cassell, Petter, Gilpin.

A FAVOURITE ALBUM OF FUN AND FANCY. *Greenaway*. London, Paris, and New York: Cassell, Petter, Gilpin.

THREE BROWN BOYS AND OTHER HAPPY CHILDREN. Ellen Haile. *Greenaway* and others. New York: Cassell.

1880 THE TWO GREY GIRLS AND THEIR OPPOSITE NEIGHBOURS. Ellen Haile. *Greenaway*. M. E. Edwards and others. New York: Cassell.

KATE GREENAWAY'S BIRTHDAY BOOK FOR CHILDREN. Verses: Mrs. Sale Barker. *Greenaway*. Routledge. Reissued 1900: Warne.

FREDDIE'S LETTER: *Stories for Little People*. Frontis.: *Greenaway* (and designs by others). Routledge.

CALENDAR FOR THE SEASONS FOR 1881. *Greenaway*. London: Marcus Ward.

c. 1880 THE OLD FARM GATE. *Stories in Prose and Verse for Little People*. *Greenaway*. M. E. Edwards and Miriam Kerns. Routledge.

1881 LONDON LYRICS. Frederick Locker. Frontis.: Randolph Caldecott; tailpiece: *Greenaway*. (London.) New York: White Stokes & Allen. (With a Greenaway bookplate design on title page.)

A DAY IN A CHILD'S LIFE. Music: Myles B. Foster (Organist of the Foundling Hospital). *Greenaway*. Eng. and printed: Edmund Evans. Routledge. Re-issued 1900: Warne.

MOTHER GOOSE, *or the Old Nursery Rhymes*. *Greenaway*. Eng. and printed: Edmund Evans. Routledge. Re-issued 1900: Warne.

1882 THE ILLUSTRATED CHILDREN'S BIRTHDAY BOOK. Edited: F. E. Weatherly. *Greenaway* and others. London: W. Mack.

1883 LITTLE ANN, *and Other Poems*. Jane and Ann Taylor. *Greenaway*. Printed: Edmund Evans. Routledge. Re-issued 1900: Warne.

ALMANACK FOR 1883. *Greenaway*. Printed: Edmund Evans. Routledge. Re-published with new text as ALMANACK FOR 1924: Warne.

A CALENDAR OF THE MONTHS, 1884. *Greenaway*. Routledge.

FLOWERS AND FANCIES, VALENTINES ANCIENT AND MODERN. R. Montgomerie Ranking and Thomas K. Tully. With four illus: *Greenaway*. (A revised edition of *The Quiver of Love*, 1877. London: Marcus Ward.)

1883 FORS CLAVIGERA. *Letters to the Workmen and Labourers of Great Britain.*
–1884 John Ruskin, LL.D. With four illus: *Greenaway*. London and Orpington: George Allen.

1884 ALMANACK FOR 1884. Kate Greenaway. Printed: Edmund Evans. Routledge.

A PAINTING BOOK. Kate Greenaway. With outlines from her various works. Routledge. Re-issued 1900 as KATE GREENAWAY'S PAINTING BOOK: Warne.

LANGUAGE OF FLOWERS. Kate Greenaway. Printed: Edmund Evans. Routledge. Re-issued 1900 and 1976: Warne.

SONGS OF THE NURSERY. *A Collection of Children's Poems*. Edited: Robert E. Mack. *Greenaway* and others. London: W. Mack.

THE ENGLISH SPELLING-BOOK. *Accompanied by a Progressive Series of Easy and Familiar Lessons*. William Mavor, LL.D. *Greenaway*. Eng. and printed: Edmund Evans. Routledge. Re-issued 1902: Warne.

1885 ALMANACK FOR 1885. Kate Greenaway. Routledge.

1885 DAME WIGGINS OF LEE *and Her Seven Wonderful Cats*. By a lady of ninety. Edited, with four additional verses, by John Ruskin, LL.D., and four additional illustrations by Kate Greenaway. London and Orpington: George Allen. (Second edition 1897.)

1885 MARIGOLD GARDEN. Pictures and Rhymes: Kate Greenaway. Printed: Edmund Evans. Routledge. Re-issued 1900: Warne.

KATE GREENAWAY'S ALBUM. Kate Greenaway. Eight copies printed: Edmund Evans. Routledge.

KATE GREENAWAY'S ALPHABET. Capital letters taken from THE ENGLISH SPELLING-BOOK and coloured. Routledge.

1886 ALMANACK FOR 1886. Kate Greenaway. Printed: Edmund Evans. Routledge. Re-issued 1900: Warne.

A APPLE PIE. Kate Greenaway. Eng. and Printed: Edmund Evans. Re-issued 1900: Warne.

THE QUEEN OF THE PIRATE ISLE. Bret Harte. *Greenaway*. Eng. and printed: Edmund Evans. London: Chatto & Windus. Boston and New York: Houghton Mifflin. Re-issued 1900: Warne.

BABY'S BIRTHDAY BOOK. *Greenaway* and others. London: Marcus Ward.

141

From *The English Spelling Book* (1884).

From *Dame Wiggins of Lee* (1885).

From *Kate Greenaway's Alphabet* (1885).

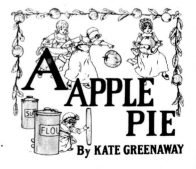

Cover design for *A Apple Pie* (1886).

From Queen Victoria's Jubilee Garland 1887

ACKNOWLEDGEMENTS

The definitive biography, *Kate Greenaway*, by M. H. Spielmann and G. S. Layard was published in 1905 by Adam and Charles Black, London. Miss Greenaway's correspondence, autobiographical notes, her records, and several firsthand recollections of friends and acquaintances were admirably compiled and documented in that volume. No new biography could possibly be attempted without reference to it.

Other sources of information for the present work have been the books, magazines, and newspapers noted with various quotations throughout the text (such as *The Times, The New York Times, The Queen*). In addition, *The Critic* (1885), *The Pall Mall Budget* (1891), *The Studio* (particularly the special number of 1894, the first art book in which Kate Greenaway's work was reproduced), should be mentioned, also *The Tatler* (1901), *The Literary Digest* (1901), *Century Magazine* (1907), *Woman's Home Companion* (1911), *Apollo* (1946), *American Antiques Journal* (1949), and *Hobbies* (1950–1953), all of which periodicals also ran articles or features on Kate Greenaway in the year indicated in parenthesis.

Useful in checking rare and generally unknown early books in which Greenaway illustrations appeared was the list of *The Kate Greenaway Collection of Miss M. I. Meacham*, sold at the Anderson Galleries, New York, in December 1921. Acknowledgement must also be made to H. M. Cundall's "appreciation" in *Kate Greenaway's Pictures from Originals Presented by Her to John Ruskin and Other Personal Friends* (1921), to *Kate Greenaway* (British Artists Series) by M. H. Spielmann, to *Art at Auction 1970–1971*, and to *Victorian Illustrated Books by Percy Muir* (1971).

I am most grateful for the help, in London, of Harriet Bridgeman, Peter Wilson, and Rodney K. Engen (Mr. Engen and I met after both, unknown to the other, had just turned in virtually complete Kate Greenaway manuscripts to our own respective publishers).

I am also deeply indebted to the staffs of the following museums and libraries with Kate Greenaway collections: Keats House, Camden (particular thanks to Miss Christina M. Gee); The Victoria and Albert Museum, London; The Royal Albert Memorial Museum, Exeter; The Detroit Public Library Rare Book Collection, Michigan, with its John S. Newbery Gift Collection of Kate Greenaway (particular thanks to Miss Gloria Francis), the Pierpont Morgan Library, New York City; and the Toronto Public Library, Canada. I am more than grateful to Anne Emerson, Cyril Stevens, and their colleagues at Frederick Warne & Co., Ltd., London, for opening up their files and giving other active assistance, as I also am grateful to my dear family and to all my colleagues at Viking Penguin Inc., New York.

From *Language of Flowers* (1884).

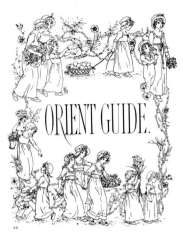

From *Orient Line Guide*
(1888).

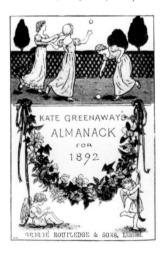

From *The Royal Progress of
King Pepito* (1889).

1886 RHYMES FOR THE YOUNG FOLK. William Allingham. Illus: Helen Allingham,
–1887 *Greenaway*, Caroline Paterson, and Harry Furniss. Eng. and Printed: Edmund
Evans. London, Paris, New York, and Melbourne: Cassell.

1887 ALMANACK FOR 1887. Kate Greenaway. Routledge. Republished with new text
as ALMANACK FOR 1925: Warne.
QUEEN VICTORIA'S JUBILEE GARLAND. Made up of Greenaway illustrations already published. Printed: Edmund Evans. Routledge.

1888 ORIENT LINE GUIDE. *Chapters for Travellers by Sea and Land.* Edited by
W. J. Loftie, B.A., F.S.A. Title page illus.: *Greenaway*. London: Sampson,
Low, Marston, Searle & Rivington.
ALMANACK FOR 1888. Kate Greenaway. Routledge.
THE PIED PIPER OF HAMELIN. Robert Browning. *Greenaway*. Eng. and printed:
Edmund Evans. Routledge. Re-issued 1903: Warne.
AROUND THE HOUSE. *Stories and Poems. Greenaway.* (From *Little Folks*, the
Illustrated London News, etc.) New York: Worthington & Co.

1889 ALMANACK FOR 1889. Kate Greenaway. Printed: Edmund Evans. Routledge.
KATE GREENAWAY'S BOOK OF GAMES. Printed: Edmund Evans. Routledge.
Re-issued 1927: Warne.
THE ROYAL PROGRESS OF KING PEPITO. Beatrice F. Cresswell. *Greenaway*. Eng.
and printed: Edmund Evans. London and Brighton: Society for Promoting
Christian Knowledge. New York: E. and J. B. Young & Co.

1890 ALMANACK FOR 1890. Kate Greenaway. Eng. and printed: Edmund Evans.
Routledge. Republished with new text as ALMANACK FOR 1926: Warne.

1891 KATE GREENAWAY'S ALMANACK FOR 1891.
–1895 KATE GREENAWAY'S ALMANACK FOR 1892.
KATE GREENAWAY'S ALMANACK FOR 1893.
KATE GREENAWAY'S ALMANACK FOR 1894. (Republished with new text as
ALMANACK FOR 1928: Warne.)
KATE GREENAWAY'S ALMANACK FOR 1895. (All five of the above Almanacks:
Greenaway. Routledge.)

1897 KATE GREENAWAY'S ALMANACK AND DIARY FOR 1897. London: J. M. Dent.
(Republished with new text as KATE GREENAWAY'S ALMANACK AND DIARY
FOR 1929: Warne.)

1898 KATE GREENAWAY'S CALENDAR FOR 1899. Routledge.

1900 THE APRIL BABY'S BOOK OF TUNES. *With the Story of How They Came to Be
Written.* By the author of *Elizabeth and Her German Garden* (Countess Von
Arnim). *Greenaway*. Macmillan.

Periodicals

1868–1873 *The People's Magazine.* London.
1874–1880 *Little Folks.* (Serialization of POOR NELLY
and other stories.) London.
1874   *Cassell's Magazine* (vol. 9). London.
1874–1886 *Illustrated London News.* London.
1877–1882 *St. Nicholas. Scribner's Illustrated Magazine for Boys and Girls.* New York.
1877–1886 *The Graphic.* London.
1879–1882 *Routledge's Every Girl's Annual.* London.
1880–1889 *Little Wide-Awake.* London.
1880   *Happy Days: The Little Folks' Annual.*
London.
1882   *Routledge's Christmas Number.* (Frontispiece) London.
1883   *The Magazine of Art.* London.
1886–1902 *The Girl's Own Paper* and *The Girl's Own
Annual.* London.
1889   *Holly Leaves* (Christmas Number). London.
1894   *The English Illustrated Magazine* (Christmas Number). London.
1884–1896 *The Ladies' Home Journal.* Philadelphia.

Title page from *Almanack for 1892.*